*from*

# MALKA'S
## KOSHER KITCHEN

*to the kitchen of*

# MALKA'S
## KOSHER KITCHEN

# MALKA'S
## KOSHER KITCHEN

*Easy Step-by-Step Recipes*
*for the Whole Year*

### Malka Engel-Padwa

FELDHEIM PUBLISHERS
JERUSALEM · NEW YORK

ISBN 1-58330-451-7

First published 2001
Copyright © 2001 by Malka Engel-Padwa

FELDHEIM PUBLISHERS
POB 35002 / Jerusalem, Israel
202 Airport Executive Park
Nanuet, NY 10954

www.feldheim.com

*Printed in Israel*

# F O R E W O R D

*To you, dear balebuste,*

*Cooking and baking are among my favorite pastimes and I am always on the lookout for new and innovative ideas in food preparation. Over the years I have published recipes in the bi-monthly "Koopjes" magazine in Antwerp as well as in other publications. The warm feedback and enthusiasm from Jewish housewives reinforced the need for clear instructions and attractive presentation. It therefore gives me great pleasure to present this cookbook, a selection of my recipes for the Jewish year, to a wider public. To ensure successful results, many a long hour has been spent rigorously testing and refining these recipes and making them easy to follow and prepare.*

*It is my hope that this book will provide you with many hours of pleasure in the kitchen, which in turn will enhance your table and bring pleasure to your family and guests. This will be my greatest reward.*

*Most of the recipes are my own. Some I remember from my grandmothers, while others are from other family members and friends. I would indeed like to take this opportunity to thank them all. I would also like to express my gratitude to my daughter Chavi for her indispensable contribution to the manuscript, and last but not least to my husband, without whose help and unflagging support the publication of this book would never have been possible.*

*Malka Engel-Padwa*

# SEPARATING CHALLAH

It is a mitzvah to separate a small portion of dough (called *challah*) that has been made with flour of one of the five grains: wheat, barley, spelt, rye, and oats. In the time of the Temple, this is given to the Kohen; nowadays it is burned or discarded.

There are different halachic opinions regarding the amount of flour in a dough which obligates one to separate *challah*, and the amount which obligates one to recite the blessing. A rabbi should be consulted for these questions and for guidance in all the details of this mitzvah.


# INSPECTING FOODS
# FOR WORMS AND INSECTS

The Torah prohibits the consumption of insects and worms. Therefore, one should carefully check fruits, vegetables, legumes, and grains, before eating them or cooking with them. Likewise, flour can require sifting. Certain fish must also be checked.

Since there are different halachic opinions regarding appropriate cleaning and inspection methods, one should consult a rabbi for detailed, practical guidance in this matter.

# NOTES AND TIPS

Before you start, read through the whole recipe and prepare all the ingredients and utensils you will need. For best results, take your time and do not rush. These helpful hints will be welcome.

* Sunflower oil has a mild, pleasant flavor and suits all dishes.
* A sugar cube is equivalent to 6 grams.
* A cup is 200 cc.
* The eggs in my recipes are large eggs, approximately 60 grams.
* One tablespoon is equivalent to 10 -12 grams.
* One teaspoon is equivalent to 5 grams.
* A package of vanilla is equivalent to 10 grams.
* A package of baking powder is equivalent to 20 grams.
* A package of yeast is equivalent to 42 grams.
* One cup of flour is equivalent to 120 grams.
* When baking powder is used, it is advisable to mix it with the flour first.
* Sifted flour makes pastries lighter.
* Margarine and eggs should be at room temperature before use.
* When beaten egg white is the last ingredient to be added to a batter, whisk the egg whites at the last minute, right before adding them.
* Dip knife into flour before cutting unbaked pastry.
* When cutting cake, dip knife into boiling water first.
* Cut margarine into pieces before kneading into dough.
* Always cover any dough that has been set aside, to prevent it from drying out.
* Add a pinch of salt and sugar to beaten egg that is brushed on pastry, in

order to improve the glaze.

❀ Allow cakes to cool for ten minutes before removing them from the pan, to prevent breaking. Cool on a cake cooling rack.

❀ To remove honey from jar easily, dip spoon into hot water first.

❀ In recipes that call for zucchini, any summer squash can be used.

# CONTENTS

## TRADITIONAL SHABBOS & YOM TOV

## PESACH

# MALKA'S
## KOSHER KITCHEN

# A P P E T I Z E R S

Special herring salad

Chopped herring

Delicious egg pâté

Eggplant paste

Chicken livers with tomatoes

Chopped liver

Light mayonnaise

Marinated herring

## SPECIAL HERRING SALAD

5 Maatjes herrings

2 shallots

1 sour apple

3 tablespoons vinegar

1 tablespoon sugar

4 generous tablespoons mayonnaise

1 tablespoon ketchup

salt and black pepper to taste

Cut the herring into very small pieces.
Chop the shallots and the apple finely and
mix all the ingredients together well.
Store in a glass jar in the refrigerator.

## CHOPPED HERRING

500 g jar pickled herring

3 schmaltz herrings

3 pickled cucumbers

1 shallot

3 hard-boiled eggs

1 sour apple

1 tablespoon matzo meal

2 tablespoons vinegar

2 tablespoons mayonnaise

Mince first six ingredients and add the
liquid from the pickled herring. Add vinegar,
mayonnaise, and matzo meal. Mix together.
Keep refrigerated.

## DELICIOUS EGG PÂTÉ

100 g margarine

2 medium onions

2 hard-boiled eggs

60 g walnuts

salt, pepper and paprika
to taste

Chop the onion finely and sauté in the margarine for half an hour on a low flame. Make a smooth paste of the onions, eggs, walnuts and spices in a blender or hand grinder.

This pâté is good for spreading on toast or for stuffing tomatoes, hard-boiled eggs, and green peppers.

Keeps for a few days in the refrigerator.

## EGGPLANT PASTE

1 medium onion

1 clove garlic

1 eggplant of
approximately 300 g

2 hard-boiled eggs

salt and pepper to taste

oil

Chop the onion finely and sauté in a little oil together with the garlic. Peel the eggplant and dice. Add to the onion, cover the pan, and sauté for 15 minutes. Add salt and pepper. Stir occasionally.

Put the eggplant mixture in a blender with the hard-boiled eggs and reduce to a smooth paste.

**TIP:** Serve on a lettuce leaf or use as a sandwich filling.

*Delicious egg pâté*

# CHICKEN LIVERS WITH TOMATOES

1/2 kg chicken livers
3 onions
2 or 3 cloves of garlic
3 tomatoes
salt, sugar and pepper to taste

Peel the onions and slice into rings. Fry together with the garlic in a little oil until golden brown.

Cut the liver into small pieces and add to the onions and garlic in the pan. Sauté for 10 minutes.

Cook together for a few minutes, stirring occasionally to prevent burning. Season with salt, sugar and pepper. Slice the tomatoes thinly and arrange on top of the mixture. Simmer for a further 15 minutes.

I got this recipe from my Aunt Zipi, who always served it as a first course on Purim.

# CHOPPED LIVER

250 g chicken liver

2 hard-boiled eggs

2 boiled potatoes

2 large onions

salt, pepper and paprika to taste

Sauté the chopped onion in oil. Cut up the liver and add to the pan. Sauté for ten minutes uncovered, stirring occasionally. Add salt, pepper and paprika to taste. Put all the ingredients into a blender to make a smooth paste.

**TIP:** Can be used as a first course or as a filling for omelettes.

# LIGHT MAYONNAISE

**PART I**

1 cup water

2 tablespoons cornstarch

pinch of salt and sugar

1/2 bottle cap acetic acid
(kosher concentrated vinegar)

Put everything except for the cornstarch and 1/4 of the cup of water into a small pan and bring to the boil. Mix the cornstarch with the remaining water and add to the pan while stirring, until it thickens. Turn off the stove, and then start immediately on the next part.

**PART II**

1 egg

1 hard-boiled egg yolk

1 tablespoon mustard

1 teaspoon sugar

1/2  teaspoon salt

1 bottle cap acetic acid
(kosher concentrated vinegar)

2 cups oil (sunflower)

Mix everything except the oil in a blender, and blending slowly, add the oil and the warm mixture. Keeps well in the fridge. Uses a third less oil than regular mayonnaise.

# MARINATED HERRING

5 pickling herrings
3 onions
3 bay leaves
1 teaspoon peppercorns
1 1/4 cups vinegar
1/4 cup water
1/2 cup sugar

Wash the herrings well and soak for 24 hours in cold water, changing the water twice (milder herrings may need only a short soaking). Cut the herrings into thick slices. Peel the onions and cut into rings. Layer the herring and the onions in a jar. Add the peppercorns and the bay leaves. Boil the water, vinegar and sugar until the sugar has dissolved, then leave to cool. Pour over the herrings, cover, and refrigerate for two or three days before using.

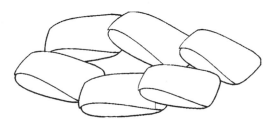

# Notes

# S O U P S

Resi's special cream soup

Créme de la reine

Special vegetable soup

Mushroom soup with rice

Mushroom soup

Tomato soup

Red lentil soup

Winter soup

Barley soup

## RESI'S SPECIAL CREAM SOUP

1 kg zucchini, unpeeled

1 piece of celery root

6 cloves of garlic

5 tablespoons uncooked oatmeal

1 teaspoon salt

1 tablespoon soup powder

6 cups water

oil

Lightly brown chopped garlic in a pan with a little oil. Add the oatmeal and stir.
Cut the well-washed zucchini into pieces and add to the pan together with the celery root and the other ingredients.
Simmer for approximately half an hour.
Remove the celery root and blend the rest until smooth.

**TIP:** Freezes well.

## CRÉME DE LA REINE

300 g parsnips

500 g zucchini

3 fine leeks (white part only)

2 medium potatoes

2 cloves of garlic

9 cups water

1 teaspoon salt

pepper to taste

1 tablespoon soup powder

parsley

Peel and cut all the vegetables into small pieces. Add remaining ingredients except parsley and cook for half an hour.
Blend in a mixer or liquidizer.
Add chopped parsley before serving.
This soup is perfect for special occasions.

**TIP:** Grated parboiled carrots can be added to this soup.

27

# SPECIAL VEGETABLE SOUP

**PART I**

1 onion

1 clove of garlic

2 carrots

2 leeks (white part)

1 piece celery root

2 tablespoons rice

250 gr mushrooms

salt

1 tablespoon soup powder

5 cups water

This soup is made in two separate parts, which are mixed together after cooking.

Peel and chop the onion and garlic and sauté in a little oil. Peel and dice the carrots. Slice the leek thinly and add to the pan with the peeled celery root and rice, and sauté for a few minutes. Add water and cook gently for 15 minutes. Add the sliced mushrooms, salt, and soup powder and cook for a further 15 minutes. Remove the celery root.

**PART II**

1 kg zucchini, unpeeled

1 onion

2 cloves garlic

1 piece celery root

50 g dill or parsley

salt

1 tablespoon soup powder

7 cups water

Wash and slice the zucchini.
Cook all ingredients together for half an hour. Remove the celery root after cooking. Blend finely and mix the two soups together.

## MUSHROOM SOUP WITH RICE

1 onion

2 cloves garlic

4 carrots

1 piece of celery root

100 g rice

500 g mushrooms

1 level teaspoon salt

1 heaped tablespoon
soup powder

pinch of paprika

10 cups water

oil

Chop the onion and garlic finely and sauté in oil. Dice the carrots and add to the pan with the celery root and sauté for ten minutes. Add rice and seasonings and mix well; then add the water. Simmer for approximately 15 minutes. Slice the mushrooms and add, and cook for a further 15 minutes. Remove the celery root.

# MUSHROOM SOUP

1 kg mushrooms

4 fine leeks (white part)

1 piece celery root

2 onions

5 cloves garlic

salt, pepper,

1 tablespoon soup powder (optional)

10 glasses water

oil

croutons

Sauté the chopped onion and garlic in a little oil until golden brown. Wash the leeks, slice into rings and add to the onion. Add the celery root and sauté for 15 minutes. Clean and slice the mushrooms and add to the pan with 10 cups of water. Cook for 20 to 25 minutes.

Add salt, pepper and soup powder. Blend to a fine purée. You can remove the celery root before blending.

Serve with croutons.

## TOMATO SOUP

15 g margarine

1 chopped onion

1 clove garlic

2 tablespoons flour

1/2 teaspoon salt

pepper to taste

2 cubes sugar

1 tablespoon soup powder (parve)

1 kg eating tomatoes, peeled (soak for 1 minute in boiling water to remove skins easily)

6 glasses water

Sauté onion and garlic lightly in margarine. Add the flour and continue sautéing for one minute while mixing. Add the other ingredients. Bring to the boil and simmer, covered, on a low flame for 20 minutes. Blend with a hand blender.

**TIP:** Delicious with Soup nockerlach (see index).

## RED LENTIL SOUP

1 onion
2 cloves garlic
1 cup lentils
1 piece celery root
4 carrots
4 medium potatoes
10 cups water
salt and pepper to taste
1 tablespoon soup powder
oil

Chop the onions and garlic finely and sauté in a little oil. Rinse the lentils in hot water, drain, and add to the pan together with the celery root and 5 cups of water. Bring to a boil, cover, and simmer for 20 minutes. Peel the carrots and potatoes, grate coarsely, and add to the soup together with the remaining 5 cups of water, salt, pepper, and soup powder and cook for a further 30 minutes. Remove the celery root.

# WINTER SOUP

1 onion

1 clove garlic

2 carrots

5 medium potatoes

6 cups water

5 tablespoons frozen peas

1 tablespoon soup powder

salt to taste

5 beef or soya sausages

oil

Chop the onion and garlic finely and sauté together in a little oil. Grate the carrots, dice the potatoes and add to the pot. Stir for a while, then add the water. Bring to a boil, and cook for approximately 30 minutes. Add the peas, soup powder and salt and cook for a further 5 minutes. Before serving, slice the sausages thinly and add to the soup.

**TIP:** Delicious with French bread.

# BARLEY SOUP

**PART I**

1/2 cup pearl barley

1 onion

1 piece celery root

1 clove garlic

2 cups water

salt

Soak the barley in water for 1 hour, drain and rinse well. Cook all the ingredients in 2 cups of water for approximately half an hour, skimming the froth off the top of the soup as it boils. Remove the onion and celery root.

**PART II**

1 zucchini (unpeeled)

1 turnip

1 piece celery root

1 piece parsnip

2 to 3 carrots

dill

2 cloves garlic

1 tablespoon soup powder

7 cups water

salt and pepper to taste

Grate all the vegetables finely (leave the dill whole). Cook with 7 cups of water, salt and pepper for 30 minutes. Remove the dill and combine with the first part of the soup.

*Créme de la reine*
*Tomato soup*

# Notes

## F I S H

Gefilte fish

Stuffed carp

Stuffed salmon

Poached trout

Poached salmon

Fish balls in tomato sauce

Fish in hot tomato sauce

Suri's tuna patties

Cod in wine

# GEFILTE FISH

### FISH MIXTURE

1 kg minced white fish
(whiting, halibut, etc.)

2 tablespoons minced onion

2 level teaspoons salt

pepper to taste

7 tablespoons sugar

2 tablespoons ground almonds

3 tablespoons matzo meal

2 to 3 large eggs

1 tablespoon oil

Other fish mixtures that can be used

1) 250 g halibut
   250 g cod
   500 g carp (Victoria)

2) 500 g carp
   500 g perch (here you might wish to add
   another egg)

Combine all ingredients and knead well by hand or use a mixer to get a fine texture. Take 2 sheets of greaseproof paper (30 cm x 40 cm) and moisten them thoroughly. Divide the fish mixture into 2 parts and roll up in the paper into salami-shaped rolls.

### STOCK (FISH YOCH)
amounts per kg of fish:

4 cups water

6 tablespoons sugar

1 teaspoon salt

pinch of pepper

1 chopped onion

2 carrots

Put all the ingredients into a large pot, bring to a boil, cover, and leave to simmer for half an hour.
Add the fish rolls in the paper. They should be gently cooked for two hours. Cool and slice.

**TIP:** To freeze gefilte fish, remove paper, wrap in foil and put in plastic bag. Freeze stock separately.

*Fish in hot tomato sauce*
*Tuna patties*
*Poached trout*
*Gefilte fish*
*Stuffed carp*

## STUFFED CARP

1 carp approximately 2 kg , cut in slices (the tail can be filleted and minced)

250 g minced carp for the filling

1 tablespoon minced onion

2 tablespoons sugar

1 tablespoon matzo meal

1 tablespoon ground almonds

1/2 teaspoon salt

pinch of pepper

1/2 egg

Sprinkle the fish slices liberally with salt and set aside for a few hours. Then rinse. Mix the other ingredients together for the stuffing and fill the hollows of the slices.

**TIP:** A small piece of greaseproof paper round the filled slice of fish holds it together well while cooking and removing from the pan.

**STOCK**

6 cups water

9 tablespoons sugar

1 teaspoon salt

pinch of pepper

3 chopped onions

2 carrots

Put all ingredients in a pot and simmer for half an hour. Place the fish slices carefully into the simmering liquid side by side and cook gently for 1 1/2 hours.
Allow to cool before removing.

# STUFFED SALMON

1 kg salmon, sliced

300 g minced salmon

2 tablespoons minced onion

2 tablespoons sugar

1/2 teaspoon salt

3 tablespoons ground almonds

1 egg

2 or 3 slices of lemon

**STOCK**

4 cups water

2 carrots

1 chopped onion

1/2 teaspoon salt

pinch of pepper

5 cubes sugar

Sprinkle the salmon slices with salt and set aside for several hours.

Combine the minced fish with the other ingredients, and mix well.

Boil the stock and simmer for half an hour. Rinse the fish slices well and fill the hollows with the minced fish mixture. Place them carefully into the simmering stock.

Form the remaining mixture into small balls, add to the pan and cook for half an hour.

Remove from heat and add the lemon slices.

Remove the lemon when cool.

**TIP:** A small piece of greaseproof paper wrapped around the filled slice of fish holds it together well while cooking and removing from the pan.

## POACHED TROUT

4 medium whole trouts

3 cups water

2 chopped onions

2 carrots

1 or 2 cubes sugar

salt and pepper to taste

1 sprig of dill

Salt the trout and set aside. Put the other ingredients in a pot and cook for half an hour. Rinse the fish and poach in the liquid for 20 minutes. Remove the pot from the heat and set aside for half an hour (do not allow to cool completely). Remove the trout, place it on a piece of aluminium foil, and remove the skins carefully (they should come off easily).

Arrange the fish on a serving plate and cover with cling film to prevent drying out.

# POACHED SALMON

6 slices salmon
4 cups water
1 onion
2 carrots
4 cubes sugar
salt and pepper to taste
3 slices lemon

Sprinkle the fish with salt and set aside for an hour. Peel and cut the onion and carrots into pieces and put into a pan with the water, sugar, salt and pepper. Simmer gently for 30 minutes. Rinse the fish and carefully place slices next to one another in the liquid. Bring to a boil again, reduce the heat and simmer for 12 to 15 minutes. Remove from the heat, add the lemon to the pan and let it cool. Remove the fish when cold and place in a dish.
Garnish with the carrots.
Strain the liquid and pour over.

**TIP:** Do not overcook or the salmon will be dry.

# FISH BALLS IN TOMATO SAUCE

**FISH MIXTURE**

1 kg minced fish

3 tablespoons minced onion

2-3 tablespoons sugar

1 teaspoon salt

pinch of pepper

1 tablespoon oil

3-4 tablespoons matzo meal

2 eggs

Mix all ingredients and set aside. Meanwhile, prepare the sauce:

**SAUCE**

3 cups tomato juice

1 cup water

2 tablespoons sugar

1/2 teaspoon salt

pinch pepper

5 cloves of garlic

oil

Slice the garlic and sauté in a little oil in a large pan. Add the rest of the sauce ingredients and simmer for 15 minutes. Form fish mixture into individual oval-shaped portions and place side by side in the sauce. Cook gently for one hour.

**TIP:** Freezes very well. This fish mixture is also ideal for fried or grilled fish cakes.

# FISH IN HOT TOMATO SAUCE

*(for 2-3 people)*

1/2 kg white fish, filleted and skinned (cod, haddock, etc.)

2 large onions

5 to 6 cloves garlic

450 g can peeled tomatoes

pinch of salt and pepper

pili pili (coarsely ground chilli peppers)

oil

Cut the fish into pieces, salt and set aside. Cut the onion widthwise, then slice thickly lengthwise. Slice the garlic and fry with the onion in a little oil. Chop the tomatoes, then add to the pan with their liquid. Season to taste and simmer for ten minutes.

Rinse the fish and add to the pan. Cover and cook gently for approximately 20 minutes.

Serve hot with rice as a main dish, or cold as a side dish.

**This recipe won an award from the Antwerp Post newspaper.**

## SURI'S TUNA PATTIES

2 cans tuna in oil (190 g)
2 carrots
1 zucchini
1 onion
4 eggs
6 tablespoons matzo meal
pinch of black pepper

### Method I

Flake the tuna. Peel carrots and onion and grate coarsely together with unpeeled zucchini. Add eggs, matzo meal, and pepper. Form round balls and lay on large baking tin covered with baking parchment. Bake in preheated oven 220° C for 40 minutes. Makes approximately 15 balls.

**TIP:** Suitable as a first course, a light meal served with salads, or for a picnic.

### Method II

Peel and grind vegetables finely. Add tuna, 2 eggs, matzo meal and pepper. Form into balls and bake as above, or fry in a little oil on both sides.

**TIP:** Can be made with 1 can tuna in oil and 1 can tuna in water.

## COD IN WINE

1 kg cod slices

4 carrots

4 fine leeks (only white part)

30 g margarine

1 cup water

6 tablespoons dry white wine

2 sprigs dill

2 cubes sugar

salt and pepper to taste

Salt the fish and set aside. Peel the carrots and the leeks and slice into rings. Sauté the leeks and carrots in the margarine over a low flame. Add the water, wine, dill and spices. Bring to the boil and simmer for half an hour.

Rinse the fish well, add to the pan and let it cook for another 15 minutes.

Serve hot.

**TIP:** Delicious with mashed potatoes.

## VEAL ROLL WITH SPECIAL SAUCE

2 1/2 kg veal roll

margarine

A veal roll consists of a slice of veal stuffed with ground meat. You can either ask your butcher to prepare this for you, or prepare it yourself by putting a roll of prepared ground meat on a flat piece of veal then rolling it up and tying it with string.

Roast the roll in a hot oven (250°C) for half an hour, turning every ten minutes and basting with margarine to brown it well all over. Reduce the heat to 160°C and continue roasting for another 2 hours. Turn from time to time and pour half a cup of water over it every 40-50 minutes (3 times in all).

**SAUCE**

50 g margarine

1 tablespoon flour

2 carrots

1 onion

piece of celery root

1 tablespoon tomato paste

parsley, thyme

pinch of sugar

Peel and cut the vegetables into small pieces. Melt the margarine in a pan, add one tablespoon of flour and stir briefly over low heat.
Add the vegetables and continue to stir for a few minutes. Slowly add two cups of gravy from the meat and simmer for a short while. Add tomato paste, some parsley, thyme and a pinch of sugar.
Cover and cook gently for an hour. Strain and serve with the meat.

# MEAT & MEAT DISHES

## CANARD À L'ORANGE

1 large duck (more than 2 kg)
pepper, paprika
1 cup orange juice
3/4 cup dry wine

Cut the duck into quarters. Put into a skillet with a little oil, and brown. Remove the duck, and pour out the oil. Sprinkle the pieces with paprika and pepper and return to the pan. Pour the juice and wine over the duck and simmer, covered, on a low flame for approximately 2 hours.

Transfer the cooking juices to a small pan, and boil uncovered to reduce the liquid. You can then thicken it by stirring in a tablespoon of cornstarch mixed with 2 tablespoons of water.

**TIP:** When cooking ducks, use large ones; otherwise you will be left with almost nothing but skin and bones.

## STUFFED DUCK

1 large duck (more than 2 kg)
pepper
1 onion
1 cup rice
1/2 cup light raisins
1 peeled apple, diced
1 cup fresh orange juice
3/4 cup water

Clean the duck and dry with absorbent paper towel. Sprinkle inside and outside with pepper.

Chop the onion and fry until golden brown. Add half the juice, the rice, raisins and apple to the frying pan and stir for one minute. Set aside until all the liquid is absorbed. Stuff the duck with this mixture and close up the opening.

Place the stuffed duck in a roasting pan or baking dish, pour the water over it and roast in a hot oven at 200°C for 30 minutes. Reduce temperature to 180°C, cover with aluminum foil, and bake for another hour. Remove foil, pour over the rest of the orange juice and roast for a further 30 minutes.

Duck dishes are very festive and highly suitable for parties and special occasions.

## CHICKEN IN WINE

4 chicken quarters

3 fine leeks

2 carrots

1 onion

2 cloves garlic

250 g mushrooms (optional)

1 teaspoon soup powder

1/4 cup wine

oil

salt, paprika

Brown the chicken with a little oil. Remove from the pan. Cut the white section of the leek, carrots, onion and garlic into small pieces and add to the pan with the soup powder. Sprinkle the chicken with paprika and put it into the pan with the vegetables. Cover the pan and simmer for an hour and 15 minutes. Now add the sliced mushrooms and the wine and simmer, covered, for another 30 minutes.

The sauce can be thickened with a tablespoon of cornstarch mixed with a tablespoon of water.

Serve hot.

**This recipe won a prize in a competition in Israel.**

## STUFFED CHICKEN QUARTERS

4 chicken quarters

1 onion

100 g stale challah or white bread

75 g flour

salt and pepper to taste

1 teaspoon soup powder

1 egg

oil

ground paprika

garlic powder

Chop the onion and fry in a little oil. Soak the challah or bread in water, and squeeze well to remove excess liquid. Finally, chop the onion and add to the bread. Mix in the flour, salt, pepper, soup powder and egg. Carefully lift the skin from edge of the chicken pieces and place a small amount of the stuffing mixture inside. Sprinkle the chicken with paprika and garlic powder. Bake at 180-200°C for 1 hour and 45 minutes.

**TIP:** Any leftover stuffing mixture can be frozen for later use or alternatively rolled up in aluminium foil and cooked in the cholent. The stuffing makes the chicken brown much more quickly, so keep an eye on it and cover with foil if necessary.

## SPECIAL OCCASION CHICKEN

4 chicken quarters

honey

1 can pineapple slices in pineapple juice, drained

4 prunes

Clean the chicken and dry with absorbent paper towel. Drizzle 1/2 teaspoon of honey over each portion. Top with a slice of pineapple with a prune in the center. Roast for 1 hour and 45 minutes in a preheated oven at approximately 200°C.

## MARINATED ROAST CHICKEN

4 chicken quarters

1/4 cup oil

paprika

2 cloves crushed garlic

Mix the oil, paprika and garlic in a large bowl. Marinate the chicken quarters in this sauce overnight.
Bake in a preheated oven at 200°C for approximately 1 hour 45 minutes.

**TIP:** Freezes very well.

*Meat loaf with red pepper*
*Chicken with sesame seeds*
*Stuffed duck*

## CHICKEN WITH SESAME SEEDS

6 chicken quarters
2 tablespoons dry white wine
2 tablespoons clear honey
1 heaping tablespoon ketchup
pinch of black pepper
sesame seeds

Mix the wine, honey, ketchup, and pepper together in a large bowl.

Spread the mixture onto each piece of chicken and leave them in the bowl to marinate overnight. Shake bowl from time to time.

Sprinkle each portion generously with sesame seeds and arrange in roasting pan. Add the leftover marinade and bake in preheated oven 180°C for approximately 1 hour and 45 minutes. Cover chicken with aluminum foil after 1 hour to prevent burning.

Strain the sauce, and boil rapidly to reduce the liquid by a quarter.

**TIP:** Delicious served with rice or mashed potatoes.

## CHICKEN GIBLETS WITH MEATBALLS

**PART I**

1 kg giblets

1 large onion

3-4 cloves garlic

1/2 cup water

1 teaspoon soup powder

2 teaspoons cornstarch
(mixed with 2 tablespoons
water)

paprika to taste

oil

Sauté the chopped onion and garlic in a pan with a little oil. Add the giblets, cover, and simmer on low heat for 1 1/2 hours. Add the water with the cornstarch, soup powder and paprika.
Add meatballs as described below.

**PART II**

1/2 kg chopped veal
or chicken

1 tablespoon oil

1 tablespoon matzo meal

salt and pepper

1 egg

Mix all the ingredients together and form into small balls. Add to the pan and cook for a further 30 minutes.

**TIP:** Delicious served with rice, pasta or mashed potatoes.

## HOLOPSHES (STUFFED CABBAGE)

1 large cabbage

**FILLING**
(sufficient for approximately
25 leaves)
1 kg ground beef
2 eggs
1 tablespoon soup powder
1 cup long-grain rice
2 cups water
1 onion
oil

**SAUCE**
2 cups tomato juice
5 cups water
3 tablespoons sugar
2 teaspoons salt
1/2 teaspoon black pepper
5 tablespoons oil
1 tablespoon vinegar

Freeze cabbage in advance.

Take out cabbage from freezer and plunge straight into a pot of boiling water. Remove leaves immediately and rinse with cold water. Place in colander to drain. Boil rice in water for five minutes, then rinse with cold water and drain. Chop onion finely and sauté in a little oil. Mix together all ingredients for filling. Place a spoonful of filling onto the thick part of each leaf (trimming away some of the thickest part of the leaves makes them more flexible). Fold over once, then fold outer edges towards center to seal in meat, then roll up in parcels. Line bottom of pot with some of the leftover cabbage. Place stuffed cabbage rolls on top. Cover with another layer of shredded cabbage and repeat until finished. Combine all ingredients for sauce in a bowl and mix well. Pour over cabbage. Cover and bring to a boil on a high flame. Turn down flame, and simmer on medium or low heat for approximately six hours.

**TIP:** Holopshes should simmer at a constant heat. Flame may need adjusting during cooking. Serve hot. These freeze well.

## MEATBALLS IN SWEET AND SOUR PINEAPPLE SAUCE

250 g ground beef

250 g ground veal

2 eggs

2 tablespoons matzo meal

pinch of pepper

1 teaspoon soup powder (optional)

1 tablespoon ketchup

Mix all the ingredients together.
Form into small balls and fry in a little oil.
They do not have to be completely
cooked through.

**SAUCE**

500 g can pineapple in pineapple juice

1 teaspoon sugar

2 tablespoons ketchup

Purée the pineapple with the juice. Add
sugar and ketchup and bring to the boil.
Add the meatballs and simmer for 15
minutes. Mix a tablespoon of cornstarch
with a tablespoon of water and use to
thicken the sauce.

**TIP:** Delicious served with rice.
Freezes well.

## MEAT LOAF

1 kg ground beef
2 or 3 eggs
2 tablespoons matzo meal
1 tablespoon soup powder
1 tablespoon oil
2 tablespoons ketchup

Mix all the ingredients together and form into two long loaves. Grease two deep aluminium baking pans 20 cm long. Put the loaves in and brush with oil. Bake in a preheated oven at 200°C for 30 minutes. Turn meat loaf over and brush with oil and bake for a further 30 minutes.
Turn off oven and leave the meat loaves to cool for 10 minutes before removing.

**TIP:** Can be served hot or cold. Delicious in sandwiches.
Perfect for vacuum packing and taking on a trip. Freezes well.

# MEAT & MEAT DISHES

## MEAT LOAF WITH RED PEPPER

1/2 kg ground beef
1/2 kg ground veal
3 or 4 eggs
4 tablespoons matzo meal
1 tablespoon soup powder
1 red bell pepper, diced
pinch of salt
1 onion, chopped
oil

Sauté the onion in a little oil. Add the diced pepper and a pinch of salt. Sauté for 15 minutes. Cool.

Add the sautéed vegetables to all the other ingredients, mix well, and put into a greased 25 cm loaf pan. Bake at 200°C for 1 1/2 hours. You can turn the loaf over while baking and sprinkle with a little oil. If making two smaller loaves, reduce the baking time by approximately 20 minutes.

**TIP:** Can be served hot or cold. Freezes well.

## BATTER FOR FRIED SCHNITZEL (CUTLETS) OR FISH

1/2 cup flour

1/2 cup water

1 teaspoon baking powder

1 egg

Mix first three ingredients, then add the egg. Set aside the mixture for approximately half an hour.

This is sufficient to coat approximately 10 schnitzels.

Enhance the taste of the schnitzel by rubbing it first with lemon.

Fish can be prepared the same way.

# Notes

# SIDE DISHES & SALADS

Bubbe Tobe's kasha with varenishkes
Gita's shlishkes
Bourekas
Mashed potatoes
Kraut pletzels
Kohlrabi with noodles
Soya shoots with mushrooms
Cooked chicory
Zucchini in tomato sauce
Carrot & fruit purée
Ratatouille
Zucchini with peppers
Rice latkes
Oriental eggplant
Cabbage salad
Letcho
Chalamade
Chrein
Beet salad
Cucumber salad
Pickled radishes
Brayne's carrot & pineapple salad
Chicory salad
Spring salad
Spring salad with avocado
Resi's sweet and sour salad (for Shabbos)
Salmon salad

# SIDE DISHES & SALADS

## BUBBE TOBE'S KASHA WITH VARENISHKES

1 cup kasha
(buckwheat groats)

2 cups hot water

salt

250 g package wide noodles

1 onion

oil

salt to taste

Fry the kasha in a pan with a little oil. Add the water and a pinch of salt.

Simmer until the water is completely absorbed (approximately 20 minutes).

Cook the noodles and drain. Chop the onion and sauté in a little oil.

Mix with the kasha and noodles. Salt to taste.

Serve warm.

## GITA'S SHLISHKES

1/2 kg flour

2 eggs

1 large cooked potato, mashed

2 tablespoons oil

just under 1/2 cup seltzer (soda water)

2 to 3 tablespoons breadcrumbs

oil

Mix flour, eggs, potato, oil, and seltzer. Knead into a dough. Roll into a long rope 1/2 cm thick and cut into 2 cm pieces. Drop into lightly salted boiling water and cook for 30 minutes.

Drain in a colander.

Heat some oil in a frying pan, add breadcrumbs and toast for a minute. Add the shlishkes and roll in the breadcrumbs over the flame until hot.

## BOUREKAS

1/2 kg flaky pastry

mashed potatoes (see below)

1 onion

egg

sesame seeds

Chop the onion finely and sauté in a little oil. Mix into the mashed potatoes. Roll out the pastry to 4 mm thickness. Cut into 8 cm squares. Place a tablespoon of mashed potatoes in the center of each and fold one corner over to the opposite side to form a triangle. Seal edges. Brush with beaten egg and sprinkle with sesame seeds. Bake in a hot oven at 220°C for 30 minutes.

**IMPORTANT:** Let the mashed potatoes cool completely before filling.

## MASHED POTATOES

750 g potatoes

1/4 cup of the potato water

salt and pepper to taste

50 g margarine

1 egg yolk

Peel the potatoes, and boil in salted water. Drain, but reserve 1/4 cup of the water. Mash the potatoes with the liquid and the rest of the ingredients, using a potato masher.

## KRAUT PLETZELS

1/2 white cabbage

250 g package wide noodles

oil

2 tablespoons salt

1 teaspoon sugar

paprika

Shred or cut cabbage finely. Salt and set aside for several hours. Squeeze excess liquid gently from the cabbage. Pour some oil into a pan and heat. Add the cabbage and sauté over a low flame for half an hour. Shake pan from time to time to avoid burning. Add paprika and sugar. Cook noodles, drain and mix with the cabbage. Serve hot.

This is a Hungarian speciality that goes well with meat or fish.

## KOHLRABI WITH NOODLES

2 kohlrabis

oil

salt and pepper to taste

250 g package wide noodles

Peel the kohlrabis, cut into quarters and slice very thinly. Heat some oil in a pan, add the kohlrabi and sauté for 20 minutes. Add salt, pepper and paprika.

Boil a pot of water, add some salt and cook the noodles for aproximately 5 minutes. Drain and rinse with cold water.

Mix the noodles with the kohlrabi.

Serve as a side dish with meat or fish.

# SIDE DISHES & SALADS

## SOYA SHOOTS WITH MUSHROOMS

| |
| --- |
| 1 onion |
| 2 carrots |
| 250 g soya shoots |
| 250 g mushrooms sliced |
| salt and pepper to taste |
| vinegar |
| oil |

Put the soya shoots in a bowl of water and add a dash of vinegar. Chop the onion finely and sauté in a little oil. Grate the carrots and add to the onion. Sauté for a few minutes. Remove the soya shoots from the water and add to the pan. Sauté for a further 15 minutes. Add the mushrooms and cook for five minutes. Serve hot.

**TIP:** You can also add small pieces of cooked or fried chicken.

## COOKED CHICORY

| |
| --- |
| 1/2 kg chicory |
| 1 onion |
| salt and pepper to taste |
| 1 cube sugar |
| oil |
| lemon juice |

Soak separated chicory leaves in a bowl of water with a bit of lemon juice. Chop the onion and sauté in a little oil until golden brown.
Remove the chicory from the water, cut up the leaves and add to the pan. Sauté for 20 minutes. Add salt, pepper and sugar. Cook for another 10 minutes.

## ZUCCHINI IN TOMATO SAUCE

1 medium onion

1 kg zucchini

70 gr can tomato paste

pinch of salt, pepper and sugar

oil

Chop the onion and sauté in a little oil. Peel the zucchini, slice and add to the pan. Sauté for approximately 15 minutes on a low flame, stirring occasionally. Remove from flame, add the tomato paste and seasoning. Mix well. Return to heat and simmer for a further 10 minutes.

**TIP:** Delicious with rice.

## CARROT & FRUIT PURÉE

600 g carrots

2 sour apples (Granny Smith)

1 large banana

1 1/2 cups fresh orange juice

2 tablespoons sugar

Cut the carrots, apples and banana into pieces. Put into a blender together with the orange juice and blend finely. Serve garnished with sliced orange.

*Zucchini in tomato sauce*
*Resi's sweet and sour salad*
*Brayne's carrot & pineapple salad*

## RATATOUILLE

1 onion

2 cloves garlic

1 red pepper

1 green pepper

1 zucchini

1 eggplant

70 g can tomato paste

pinch of salt, pepper and sugar

Chop the onion and garlic finely and sauté in a pan with a little oil. Dice the peppers and add to the pan. Sauté for 10 minutes. Peel the zucchini and eggplant, dice and add. Sauté for a further 20 minutes. Add the tomato paste and seasonings, and simmer for another 10 minutes.

## ZUCCHINI WITH PEPPERS

1 large onion

2 cloves garlic

2 red peppers

2 green peppers

1 kg zucchini

70 g can tomato paste

dash of oil

salt, sugar

Chop the onion and garlic finely and sauté in a pan with a dash of oil. Dice peppers and add to the pan. Sauté for 15 minutes. Peel zucchini, dice, add to the pan and cook gently for half an hour. Add a pinch of salt and sugar, and mix the tomato paste into the vegetables.
Simmer for several minutes.

## RICE LATKES

1 cup long-grain rice
1/2 cup diced carrots
1/2 cup chopped celery
1 whole egg
1 egg yolk
2 tablespoons matzo meal
1 teaspoon soup powder

Cook the rice in 2 cups of water and a teaspoon of soup powder for half an hour. Cool. Cook the carrots and celery in half a cup of water and a pinch of salt for 15 minutes and leave to cool. Mix the rice and vegetables together and add the eggs and matzo meal. Heat some oil in a pan and drop spoonfuls of the mixture into it.
Fry on both sides and serve warm.

**TIP:** Perfect on their own or as an accompaniment to a main dish.

## ORIENTAL EGGPLANT

1 kg eggplant

2 onions

2 pickled cucumbers

2 tablespoons pickled
red peppers (gamba)

3 cloves of garlic

5 tablespoons vinegar

pinch of salt and pepper

Wash the eggplants but do not peel. Dry and cut into chunks. Salt and leave for a few hours in a colander. Dry with absorbent paper towels. Peel the onions and slice into rings. Sauté some of the eggplant pieces and onions in a little oil for a few minutes and put into a dish. Repeat until they are all sautéed. Wash the garlic (do not peel) and press through a garlic press. Slice the pickles. Add to the dish together with the peppers, vinegar, salt and pepper. Shake well. Do not mix with a spoon or fork. Put into a glass jar.

Will keep in refrigerator for up to 2 weeks.

**TIP:** Delicious on bread or toast or as a side dish.

## CABBAGE SALAD

1 medium white cabbage

2 carrots (optional)

1/2 cup vinegar
or lemon juice

1 tablespoon salt

2 tablespoons sugar

5 tablespoons mayonnaise

Open the cabbage and cut away the hard stalks. Check for insects. Wash and drain in a colander. Cut finely or shred coarsely with an electric shredder. Mix the other ingredients in a bowl, pour over the cabbage and mix together.
Keep refrigerated.

## LETCHO

1/2 green pepper

1/2 red pepper

1 onion

2 beaten eggs

salt and pepper to taste

oil

Chop the onion finely and sauté in a pan with a little oil. Dice the peppers and add to the pan. Sauté for 15 minutes, stirring occasionally. Add the eggs and cook for a further 10 minutes.
Serve on toast.

# SIDE DISHES & SALADS

## CHALAMADE

| | |
|---|---|
| 1/2 small white cabbage | Shred cabbage finely. Slice the cucumber |
| 2 cucumbers | (unpeeled) and the onion. Shred the |
| 2 onions | peppers. Salt the vegetables and set aside |
| 1 red pepper | for a few hours; then squeeze out any |
| 1 green pepper | excess water. Grate the peeled carrots |
| 2 carrots | coarsely. |
| salt | |

**PICKLING LIQUID**

Bring the water, sugar, bay leaves, and vinegar to a boil. Leave to cool a little and mix with the vegetables. Pour into a glass jar and store in refrigerator.
Leave for at least one day before using.

2 1/2 cups vinegar
1 cup water
7 tablespoons sugar
bay leaves

Keeps for 2 to 3 weeks.

## CHREIN

1 kg beets

1 horseradish
(approximately 350 g)

salt and pepper to taste

2 tablespoons sugar

juice of 1 lemon or
1/3 cup vinegar

Wash the beets well and boil unpeeled for an hour. Cool, then remove peel (comes off easily). Grate the beets finely. Peel the horseradish and grate finely. Mix together all ingredients.

Keep refrigerated. Freezes well.

**TIP:** Delicious with gefilte fish, roast beef, or chicken.

## BEET SALAD

1 kg medium beets

1 onion

2 tablespoons sugar

salt and pepper to taste

juice of 1 lemon or
a 1/3 cup of vinegar

Wash the beets well and boil unpeeled for an hour, or until soft. Drain and cool completely. Peel the beets, cut into quarters and slice thinly. Chop the onion finely. Add the salt, pepper, sugar and lemon juice and mix together.
Keep refrigerated.

## CUCUMBER SALAD

1 cucumber
1 onion
1/2 red pepper
1 teaspoon salt
1/4 cup sugar
1/4 cup vinegar
or lemon juice

Slice the cucumber and the onion into rings. Dice the pepper or cut into strips. Mix the salt, sugar and vinegar together in a bowl, pour over the vegetables and mix well.

**TIP:** Peel one strip of the cucumber lengthwise, then leave a gap of equal width before peeling the next strip. Continue all the way around. The striped effect will enhance your salad.

## PICKLED RADISHES

2 bunches red radishes
3/4 cup vinegar
1/4 cup water
2 tablespoons sugar
1 teaspoon salt

Wash and cut the "tails" of the radishes off. Larger ones can be cut in half, smaller ones left whole. Put in a jar. Bring the rest of the ingredients to a boil and boil until the sugar has completely dissolved. Pour over the radishes. Leave overnight to mature.

## BRAYNE'S CARROT & PINEAPPLE SALAD

1/2 kg carrots

1 sour apple (Granny Smith)

1/2 kg can pineapple in its own juice

2 tablespoons sugar

2 tablespoons raisins (optional)

Peel carrots and apple. Grate carrots finely and shred apple coarsely. Purée the pineapple with its juice and mix with the carrots and apple. Add the sugar and the raisins.

The coarsely grated apple is appealing in appearance and taste.

## CHICORY SALAD

1/2 kg chicory

1 sour apple (Granny Smith)

2 tablespoons mayonnaise

a few drops of lemon juice

Cut the chicory finely.
Peel the apple and chop coarsely.
Add the mayonnaise and lemon juice.
Mix well.

## SPRING SALAD

2 medium potatoes, cooked
150 g can peas
150 g can sweet corn
1 tomato
1 pickled cucumber
1 head of chicory
1 onion
oil
salt to taste

Chop the onion finely.
Cut all the vegetables into small pieces.
Drain the corn and peas.
Mix together well, add some oil and salt and serve.

## SPRING SALAD WITH AVOCADO

1 medium tomato
1/2 cucumber
2 heads of chicory
1 carrot
1 avocado
300 g can sweet corn
1 onion
oil
salt to taste

Chop the onion finely, grate the carrot and cut up the rest of the vegetables finely. Drain the sweet corn, and add some oil and salt. Mix everything together.

## RESI'S SWEET AND SOUR SALAD (FOR SHABBOS)

1/2 kg cucumber
3 carrots
1 onion
1 red pepper
1 yellow pepper
1/2 cup sugar
2/3 cup lemon juice
4 level teaspoons salt
1 tablespoon oil
4 tablespoons water

Slice the cucumber, carrots and onion thinly. Shred the peppers coarsely. Mix all ingredients together and leave to marinate for at least a day before using. Keep refrigerated.

## SALMON SALAD

450 g can salmon
400 g can mixed vegetables
1 hard-boiled egg
1 pickled cucumber
1 tablespoon vinegar
3 tablespoons mayonnaise
1 teaspoon capers
salt to taste

Remove skin and bones from the salmon and flake. Chop the egg and pickle coarsely. Drain the vegetables and mix everything together. Serve as a salad.

**TIP:** For special occasions serve in a tall cup or on a lettuce leaf.

# Notes

# COMPOTES & DESSERTS

Festive fruit dessert

Stuffed dumplings

Strawberry dessert

Mixed fruit compote

Red pear compote

Mixed dried fruit compote

Summer compote

Apple compote in orange juice

Festive applesauce with meringue

Chocolate mousse

Strawberry sorbet

Vanilla ice cream

Chocolate sauce

Ice cream with liqueur & raisins

Pavlova fruit meringue

Gita's trifle

# FESTIVE FRUIT DESSERT

**PART 1**

3 cups pineapple juice

1 cup water

2 tablespoons cornstarch

**PART 2**

1/2 kg strawberries

sugar

Boil the pineapple juice and 1/2 cup of water in a pan. Mix the cornstarch with the other 1/2 cup water, then add to the hot juice, stirring until thickened. Allow to cool and store in the refrigerator. Wash and hull the strawberries. Carefully dry them with absorbent kitchen towels. Put a pan over a flame and allow it to become hot, without adding any oil.

Put in the strawberries, sprinkle a little sugar over them, and let them caramelize for 5 minutes, shaking the pan occasionally (gently, so as to keep the fruit intact; do not use a spoon). Serve the pineapple mixture in a bowl with a little of the fruit in the center.

**TIP:** You may use any other dark fruit. This is very tasty when the pineapple is cold and the strawberries hot.

## STUFFED DUMPLINGS

1/2 kg medium potatoes

25 g margarine

80 to 100 g flour

1 egg

apricot jam

220 g can apricots or peaches

1 tablespoon breadcrumbs

Cook the potatoes in their jackets for 30 minutes. Drain and peel immediately and mash with a pinch of salt and the margarine. Allow to cool down completely, then add the flour and egg and form into a long roll. Cut into 6 equal lengths and roll into balls. Make a hollow in each ball with your finger, put in some jam, then re-close. Boil some water in a saucepan and add a pinch of salt and a dash of oil. Drop the dumplings into the boiling water and cook for twenty minutes. Drain.

Before serving, heat some oil in a frying pan and add the breadcrumbs, then roll the dumplings in the crumbs and heat on all sides. Blend the apricots or peaches and serve with the dumplings.

**TIP:** The dumplings can be prepared several hours in advance and warmed up in a pan before serving.

# COMPOTES & DESSERTS

## STRAWBERRY DESSERT

1/2 kg strawberries

1 medium sized
fresh pineapple

2 ripe bananas

Wash and hull the strawberries. Peel the pineapple and cut into chunks. Peel the bananas. Blend together in a liquidizer. You can add sugar if preferred. Serve cold with a scoop of ice cream.

## MIXED FRUIT COMPOTE

1 kg strawberries

1 kg apricots

3/4 kg sweet cooking apples
(Belgian Golden)

4 cups water

Peel and core the apples, cut into pieces and cook in the water for 15 minutes. Wash the apricots, cut into pieces, add to the apples, and cook for a further 30 minutes. Remove from flame. Wash and hull the strawberries, then blend into a puree and mix into the cooked fruit.

## RED PEAR COMPOTE

1 kg pears (St. Remy)
10 tablespoons sugar
4 cups water
2 or 3 slices lemon

Peel the pears, leaving the stems. Cut large pears into 4, smaller ones in half, then remove the core. Put the pears and the sugar into the water and bring to a boil. Lower the heat, cover, and simmer gently for 5 hours. By this time the pears will have turned red. Remove from the heat and add the lemon slices.

**NOTE:** Only St. Remy pears are suitable for this compote.

*Chocolate mousse*
*Apple compote in orange juice*

## MIXED DRIED FRUIT COMPOTE

200 g prunes
200 g dried apricots
120 g dried apples
2 tablespoons sugar
3 slices lemon

Put all the fruit in a bowl of water, making sure that the fruit is covered. Soak overnight. Put the fruit with the water in which it was soaked into a pan and add another 3/4 cup of water and the sugar. Cook for ten minutes. Remove from heat and toss in lemon slices.

## SUMMER COMPOTE

1 kg apricots
1/2 kg strawberries
3/4 cup water
(use large, first-quality fruit for sweetness)

Remove the pits from the apricots and cut into pieces and wash. Put into pan with the water and bring to the boil. Reduce heat and simmer, covered, for 30 minutes. Leave to cool. Wash and hull the strawberries. With a blender or whisk blend them finely and mix into the slightly cooled apricots. It is not necessary to sweeten this compote with sugar.

## APPLE COMPOTE IN ORANGE JUICE

1 kg sour cooking apples (Rennet)

1 kg sweet cooking apples (Belgian Golden)

1 large pear

1 3/4 cups freshly squeezed orange juice

Peel and core the fruit, cut into pieces and put into a pan with the orange juice. Cover, and cook on gentle heat for around 30 minutes. Blend finely.

Freezes very well.

**TIP:** Serve garnished with a slice of orange.

## FESTIVE APPLESAUCE WITH MERINGUE

1 kg sweet cooking apples (Belgian Golden)

1/4 cup water

4 egg whites

8 tablespoons sugar

Peel and core the apples and cut into small pieces. Braise in the water on a low flame until cooked. Blend with a hand blender. Pour into a 25 x 25 cm Pyrex or ovenproof dish. Whisk the egg whites and sugar until very stiff. Spread on top of the apple mixture and bake in a preheated oven at 160°C for approximately 30 minutes. This dish can be cut into squares for serving.

# COMPOTES & DESSERTS

## CHOCOLATE MOUSSE

150 g bitter chocolate

1 1/2 tablespoons instant coffee powder

2 tablespoons boiling water

4 eggs

whipping cream for decoration

Break the chocolate into pieces and melt in a double boiler or over a basin of hot water. Mix the coffee with the water and add to the chocolate. Mix in the egg yolks one at a time. Whisk the egg whites until stiff and fold carefully into the chocolate mixture. Divide into cups and leave to set in the refrigerator. Before serving garnish with whipped cream.

## STRAWBERRY SORBET

3 egg whites

1 1/2 cups sugar

juice of 1 1/2 large lemons

2 or 3 packets vanilla sugar

500 g strawberries

Wash and hull the strawberries. Whisk the egg whites until stiff. Slowly add the sugar, vanilla and lemon juice while beating. Add the strawberries one at a time while beating. Freeze.

# COMPOTES & DESSERTS

## VANILLA ICE CREAM

10 eggs

1 1/2 cups sugar

5 packets vanilla sugar

1 cup oil
(preferably sunflower oil)

juice of 1 lemon and warm
water (1 1/2 cups in total)

Separate the eggs. Whisk the egg whites until stiff. Slowly add the sugars and egg yolks, then add the rest of the ingredients. Pour into a dish and freeze.

## CHOCOLATE SAUCE

100 g chocolate

50 g sugar

6 tablespoons water

25 g margarine

Melt the chocolate with the water and sugar over a low flame.
Remove from heat and add the margarine.
Stir well until melted.
Heat in double boiler before serving.

**TIP:** Delicious served with ice cream, blintzes, etc.

## ICE CREAM WITH LIQUEUR & RAISINS

5 eggs
3/4 cup sugar
1/2 cup oil
3/4 cup liqueur
1/2 cup raisins

Soak the raisins in the liqueur for an hour. Whisk the egg whites, adding the sugar slowly. Add the egg yolks one at a time, then the oil, and finally the raisins with liqueur. Freeze.

**TIP:** Can be served with chocolate sauce.

# PAVLOVA FRUIT MERINGUE

**PART I: MERINGUE**
(can be made a
day in advance)

3 egg whites

150 g sugar

1 packet vanilla sugar

1/2 teaspoon vinegar

2 teaspoons cornstarch

Whisk the egg whites until stiff. Slowly add the sugars. Then add the vinegar and the cornstarch. Line a baking tin with parchment paper and draw a circle of 25 cm diameter on it. Heap the meringue into this circle. Bake in a preheated oven at 140°C for 1 hour and 20 minutes.
Leave to cool in the oven.

**PART II: FILLING**

400 g whipping cream

1 tablespoon powdered sugar

1 small pineapple (you may use other fruit if you prefer)

1 papaya

2 tablespoons cognac

Cut the fruit into pieces and marinate in the cognac for 1/2 an hour. Just before serving, whip the cream and spoon onto the meringue, and arrange the fruit on top.

## GITA'S TRIFLE

**CAKE**

6 eggs

300 g flour

400 g sugar

2 packets vanilla sugar

1 packet baking powder

1 cup oil

Mix together all ingredients.
Pour into a 25 cm x 35 cm greased baking tin and bake in preheated oven at 175°C for approximately 40 minutes.

**TIP:** Any other similar cake can be used.

**FILLING AND TOPPING**

500 g strawberries

1 large can pineapple slices

3 or 4 kiwi fruit

1 packet instant strawberry jello

1 liter whipping cream

140 g sugar

wine

Wash, hull and slice the strawberries. Peel and slice the kiwi fruit. Drain the pineapple, set aside a few slices for garnishing and cut the rest into chunks. Whip the cream with the sugar. Take a large bowl and line the bottom with a layer of cake. Sprinkle with a little wine. Cover with a layer of strawberries. Dissolve two tablespoons of instant jello in a tablespoon of boiling water and pour over the strawberries. Cover with a layer of cream. Repeat, replacing the strawberries with pineapple, then again using the kiwi fruit. Cover with another layer of cake. Top with cream and garnish with slices of pineapple, kiwi fruit and strawberries.
Best if prepared on the day it is to be eaten.

# Notes

# CHEESE AND DAIRY DISHES & CHEESECAKES

Cheesecake

Cheese delkelach

Resi's dairy rogelach

Sour cream cake with cinnamon

Mme. Freund's dairy kranz

Brayne's easy cheesecake

Resi's milchig lokshen kugel

Cheese latkes

Pirogen

Mamelige

Pancakes with mushrooms

Cherry filling for pancakes

Omelette with hard cheese

Miriam's zucchini quiche

Pasta with cheese or mushroom sauce

# CHEESECAKE

**PASTRY**

1 cup flour

50 g margarine

3 tablespoons sugar

1 egg

pinch of salt

1/4 teaspoon baking powder

Mix all pastry ingredients and knead into a dough. Flatten with hands and press into the bottom of a greased baking dish, round or rectangular. Preheat oven to a high temperature (230°C).

**FILLING**

1 kg baking cheese

250 g cream

150 g powdered sugar

150 g white sugar

3 packets vanilla sugar

5 tablespoons flour

4 eggs

Mix the cheese, cream and powdered sugar together very well. Whisk the eggs, white sugar and vanilla sugar until fluffy. Fold the egg mixture carefully into the cheese mixture, slowly adding flour as well. Pour onto the pastry and place in the oven. Reduce the temperature to 160°C and bake for 1 1/2 hours. Leave the cake to cool in the oven for at least 6 hours without opening the door.

## CHEESE DELKELACH

**DOUGH**

1/2 cup warm water

1 packet yeast plus
1 teaspoon sugar

1 kg flour

pinch of salt

100 g margarine at
room temperature

2 tablespoons oil

3 eggs

5 tablespoons sugar

200 g margarine for spreading
on the pastry

flour and sugar for sprinkling

Put the water, yeast and a teaspoon of sugar into a bowl and set aside until frothy. Mix the flour, salt, margarine, oil and eggs. Add the yeast mixture, and knead into a dough. Divide into two and roll out each piece. Spread 200 g of margarine over the two pastries. Sprinkle a little flour and sugar over the margarine, fold dough up like an envelope and set aside for half an hour.

**FILLING**

1/2 kg baking cheese

2 eggs

5 tablespoons sugar

2 packets vanilla sugar

1 egg for glaze

Mix the filling ingredients together. Roll out the dough thinly and cut into 10 cm squares. Put a spoonful of filling in the centre of each square. To make each delke, bring the four corners into the center and seal the open edges. Alternatively, you can just bring two opposite corners together leaving the other two flat. Brush with beaten egg and bake in a hot oven at 220°C for 20 to 25 minutes.

## RESI'S DAIRY ROGELACH

400 g flour
150 g butter
150 g cream
1/2 cup sugar
1 egg yolk
1 cup warm milk
1/3 packet yeast
pinch of salt

**FILLING**
butter for spreading
4 packets vanilla sugar
cinnamon

Put all the ingredients except the milk and yeast in a bowl. Put the yeast in the milk with a little sugar and set aside until it begins to froth. Pour into the flour mixture and knead into a dough. Leave overnight in refrigerator. Before use, allow to reach room temperature. Divide into 4 parts. Roll out each piece into a thin circle, spread a little butter and sprinkle with a packet of vanilla sugar and some cinnamon. Cut across to form 12 triangles and roll up each one to form rogelach. Brush with beaten egg and bake in a preheated oven at 180°C for 20 minutes. These dairy rogelach are very tasty and freeze well.

## SOUR CREAM CAKE WITH CINNAMON

100 g butter
160 g sugar
1 packet vanilla sugar
2 large eggs
180 g sour cream
250 g flour
1 teaspoon baking soda

**FILLING & DECORATION**
100 g ground walnuts
100 g brown sugar
1 teaspoon cinnamon

Mix filling ingredients in a bowl and set aside.

Mix the butter, sugar and vanilla sugar and beat well. Separate the eggs. Add the egg yolks to the mixture first, one at a time, and then the whites. Mix a little; add the sour cream, flour and baking soda and mix again. Grease a 20-22 cm round baking pan. Pour in half of the batter and cover with half of the filling. Cover with the rest of the batter and then sprinkle the remaining filling on top. Bake in a preheated oven at 160°C for 1 hour. Allow the cake to cool in the pan.

# Mme. FREUND'S DAIRY KRANZ

### DOUGH

1 kg flour

1 cup warm milk

1 packet yeast

250 g butter

250 g sour cream

3 eggs

5 tablespoons sugar

pinch of salt

1 egg for glaze

### FILLING

butter for spreading

4 tablespoons cocoa

8 tablespoons sugar

pinch of cinnamon

dried coconut flakes

100 g grated chocolate

### FINAL GLAZE (OPTIONAL)

apricot jam

100 g powdered sugar

1 teaspoon glucose (if available)

2 tablespoons boiling water

Put the flour into a bowl and make a well in the center. Pour in the milk, yeast and sugar and set aside for 10 minutes. Add the rest of the ingredients and knead into a dough. Cover with a towel and allow to rise. Divide into 3 or 4 parts. Roll each part out into a square 1/2 cm thick and spread with some butter. Mix together cocoa, sugar and cinnamon and sprinkle over the squares of pastry. Sprinkle some dried coconut and grated chocolate on top. Roll up lengthwise and form each roll into a closed ring. Make small cuts into the outside at regular intervals of 2 cm. Brush with beaten egg and bake in a preheated oven at 200°C for 30 minutes.

**TIP:** For a richer finish, as soon as cake is removed from the oven, brush with apricot jam. Make a glaze by mixing powdered sugar with boiling water (and a teaspoon of glucose, if available), and brush on top of the jam.

## BRAYNE'S EASY CHEESECAKE

2 cups flour
1 teaspoon baking powder
100 g butter
5 tablespoons sugar
1 egg

Knead into a dough. Roll out 3/4 of the dough to line the bottom of a greased 35 cm x 25 cm baking pan. Flatten out the rest of the dough onto another greased baking tray and bake both in a preheated oven at 190°C for approximately 20 minutes.

**FILLING**

500 g  soft white cheese 5%
250 g whipping cream
1 cup powdered sugar
1 packet instant vanilla pudding

Mix the sugar with the cheese. Whip the cream together with the instant pudding and fold into the cheese mixture. Cover the cake in the tin with the cheese mixture and smooth over the top. Crumble the other piece of pastry and sprinkle over it .

Keep refrigerated.

*Cheesecake*
*Mme. Freund's dairy kranz*
*Miriam's zucchini quiche*

## RESI'S MILCHIG LOKSHEN KUGEL

500 g fine egg noodles
600 g soft white cheese 5%
250 g cream
pinch of cinnamon
250 g sugar
3 packets vanilla sugar
6 large eggs

Cook the noodles "al dente" (until just done) in salted water. Rinse with cold water and drain. Mix with the cheese, cream and cinnamon. Whisk the eggs with the sugars until stiff, then fold into the noodles. Pour into a well-greased 25 cm x 35 cm baking tin and bake in a preheated oven at 190°C for 1 hour and 15 minutes.

## CHEESE LATKES

250 g baking cheese
1 egg
1/4 cup sugar
1 packet vanilla sugar
pinch of cinnamon
1/4 cup flour

Mix all ingredients together well. If necessary, add a bit more flour. Form into balls and roll in breadcrumbs. Heat oil or butter in a frying pan and fry on both sides until golden brown.

## PIROGEN

**DOUGH**
1/2 kg flour
pinch of salt
1 tablespoon oil
1 egg
1 1/2 cups warm water

**FILLING**
1/2 kg baking cheese
1 egg
2 packets vanilla sugar

Combine ingredients into a hard dough. Roll out and cut out circles with the rim of a cup. Mix together ingredients for the filling. Make small balls of the filling and place one in the center of each circle. Fold the dough in half and seal the edges with fingers. Bring a pot of water to a boil together with a dash of oil and salt. Drop a few pirogen into the boiling water, one at a time. When they float to the surface, they are cooked. Remove and let the water boil again before adding more pirogen.

**TIP:** Before serving, they can be fried on both sides in a little butter, with some breadcrumbs if preferred. Pirogen can also be filled with a potato mixture (see Bourekas, pg. 70).
Freezes well.

# MAMELIGE

100 g fine cornmeal
3 1/2 cups water
1/2 teaspoon salt
hard cheese
salted white cheese
sour cream

Bring the water and salt to a boil. Add the cornmeal to the boiling water slowly, while stirring with a wooden spoon or whisk. Cover and cook for 30 minutes on a low flame, stirring occasionally. Pour a layer of this mamelige onto a dessert plate. Grate a little hard cheese onto it and cover with another layer of mamelige. Crumble some salted white cheese on top and cover with another layer of mamelige. Serve with sour cream, leben, or milk.

*I got this recipe from a friend on one of my journeys and have adapted it somewhat; it is perfect for a light meal or an in-between snack. I think you will love it.*

# PANCAKES WITH MUSHROOMS

**BATTER**

2 eggs

1 3/4 cups skim milk

180 g flour

5 tablespoons oil

pinch of salt

Mix all ingredients and set aside for half an hour. Heat a little oil in a 25 cm pan. Pour in a little batter to cover base of pan thinly and fry lightly on both sides. Repeat until all batter is finished.

**FILLING**

1 onion

250 g mushrooms (sliced)

150 g grated hard cheese

pinch of salt

Chop onion and sauté in a little oil. Add the sliced mushrooms and sauté for 3 or 4 minutes. Season to taste. Drain. Fill each pancake with mushroom and cheese mixture, and close like an envelope. Before serving fry on both sides in a pan.

**TIP:** Good served as a main dish together with carrot salad.

# CHERRY FILLING FOR PANCAKES

**FILLING**

580 g pitted Morello cherries in syrup

2 packets vanilla sugar

2 tablespoons cornstarch

powdered sugar

Drain cherries, saving syrup. Boil 1 cup of syrup with the vanilla sugar. Mix the rest of the syrup with cornstarch and add slowly to boiling syrup mixture, stirring until it thickens. Cool slightly; mix in cherries. Fill pancakes, roll up, and dust with powdered sugar.

## OMELETTE WITH HARD CHEESE

1 egg

salt and pepper to taste

1 slice hard cheese

Heat a little oil in a pan. Beat the egg with the seasonings and pour into the pan. Leave to set a little. Lay the slice of cheese on one half of the omelette then leave for a further 2 minutes. Fold, remove from pan and set out on a plate with sliced tomatoes. Serve with toast.

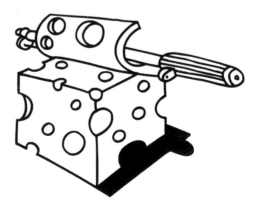

## MIRIAM'S ZUCCHINI QUICHE

1 1/2 cups flour
100 g margarine
2 tablespoons sour cream
1 egg yolk
1 teaspoon baking powder
pinch of salt

Mix all ingredients together in the given order to make a dough. Use to line a round, greased 25 cm baking dish.

**FILLING**
1 large onion
1 kg zucchini
250 g soft white cheese 5%
2 eggs
2 tablespoons mushrooms
soup powder (optional)
4 tablespoons breadcrumbs
salt to taste

Chop the onion finely and sauté in a little oil. Peel the zucchini, cut into small cubes and add to the onion. Sauté for 10 minutes. Put into a dish and allow to cool.
Then add the rest of the ingredients, mix and pour onto pastry.
Bake for 45 minutes at 200°C.

Serve hot.

**TIP:** For a variation, grate the unpeeled zucchini.

## PASTA WITH CHEESE OR MUSHROOM SAUCE

500 g package of pasta (any variety)

Cook pasta according to instructions on packet.

**CHEESE SAUCE**

20 g butter or margarine

1 tablespoon flour

2 tablespoons soft cheese

1 teaspoon mustard

salt and pepper to taste

1 cup milk

100 g grated hard cheese

Put the butter in a pan with the flour and stir until the butter has melted. Add the cheese and seasonings and then the milk. Stir over a low flame until the mixture thickens. Add the grated cheese and mix again.
Serve over the pasta.

**MUSHROOM SAUCE**

250 g mushrooms

1 onion

30 g margarine

salt, pepper and soup powder to taste

1 1/2 cups water

2 tablespoons flour

Chop the onion finely and sauté in the margarine. Slice the mushrooms and add to the pan. Sauté for 2 to 3 minutes.
Season with salt, pepper and soup powder. Mix the flour with the water and slowly add to the pan. Stir until thickened.

# Notes

# S P R E A D S  &  D R I N K S

Strawberry jam

Chocolate spread

Punch

Chocolate liqueur

Egg liqueur

## STRAWBERRY JAM

1 kg strawberries

900 g sugar

Wash and hull the strawberries and dry
with absorbent paper towel. Put the
strawberries in a saucepan with the sugar.
Bring slowly to a boil while stirring.
Cook for 15 minutes after it starts bubbling
continuously.
Cool and store in closed jars.
Keep refrigerated.

## CHOCOLATE SPREAD

3 tablespoons sugar

3 tablespoons cocoa

3 tablespoons water

3 egg yolks

125 g margarine

Mix the water, sugar and cocoa, and warm
over low heat while stirring. Cut the
margarine into small pieces and add.
As the margarine melts, add the egg yolks,
stirring all the time.
Cool and keep refrigerated.

## PUNCH

1/2 kg strawberries
450 g can apricots
1 cup white wine
2 tablespoons sugar
3 packets vanilla sugar

Blend all the ingredients until smooth. Serve in tall glasses.

**TIP:** To give the glasses a frosted appearance, before pouring in the punch put a little lemon juice in a saucer and some white sugar in another. Dip the rims of the glasses first into the juice, then into the sugar. Add the punch.

## CHOCOLATE LIQUEUR

1 kg sugar

100 g cocoa

2 teaspoons instant coffee powder

2 1/2 cups water

1 cup spirit alcohol 96°

Dissolve the sugar, cocoa and coffee in the water over a low flame, stirring until the sugar has completely dissolved. Set aside to cool. Mix in the alcohol very well then strain once or twice for a smooth finish.

## EGG LIQUEUR

2 1/2 cups sugar

3 packets vanilla sugar

2 1/2 cups water

3 egg yolks

1 tablespoon cornstarch

3/4 cup spirit alcohol 96°

Dissolve the sugars in the water, bring to a boil, then simmer over a low flame. Mix the cornstarch into the egg yolks. Remove the sugar water from the flame and stir into the egg yolk mixture. Return to the flame and reheat until it thickens, stirring all the time. Allow to cool, then add the alcohol and mix well. You might have to strain it once or twice to get a smooth liqueur.

**VARIATION:** For a chocolate flavor, add 2 teaspoons of cocoa and one teaspoon of dissolved instant coffee when boiling the water.

# Notes

# BREAD, YEAST CAKES, TARTS AND COOKIES

Egg challos
Tobi's non-egg sweet challos
Bubbe Raatze's challos
Mezoinos zemelach
Mezoinos croissant with onion
Mezoinos zemelach with raisins or chocolate chips
Crumb topping
Suri's babke
Kokosh cake
Shoshana's shoshanim
Tzop
Rogelach
Raatze's rogelach
Apple tart
Apple pie
Orangettes
Chanukah doughnuts
Honig kichelach
Hamantashen
Egg kichelach
Chocolate balls
Sesame snack
Rosettes
Refrigerator cookies (three versions)

# EGG CHALLOS

1.8 kg flour

5 cups hot water

2 packets yeast

1 cup sugar

3/4 cup oil

2 level tablespoons salt

4 egg yolks

1 egg
for brushing challos

sesame / poppy seeds

Put the flour into a bowl and make a well in the center. Pour in the water, yeast and sugar. Leave until the yeast starts to froth (approximately 10 minutes). Add the rest of the ingredients and knead into a smooth dough. Cover with a dish towel and allow to rise until it has doubled in bulk (approximately 1 hour).

Punch down and twist into your favorite challos. Place on a greased baking sheet or oven tray.

Beat an egg with a pinch of salt and sugar and brush over the challos. Sprinkle with sesame or poppy seeds and allow to rise. Bake in a preheated oven at approximately 225°C for 40 minutes.

**TIP:** After 20-25 minutes, when the challos are partially baked, you can take them out and quickly touch up any unglazed patches with egg.

All challos freeze well.

*Challos*
*Mezoinos zemelach*
*Shoshana's shoshanim*

# BREAD, YEAST CAKES, TARTS AND COOKIES

## TOBI'S NON-EGG SWEET CHALLOS

2 kg flour

5 1/4 cups hot water

2 packets yeast

1 1/2 cups sugar

1 cup oil

2 level tablespoons salt

Prepare as for Egg Challos.

## BUBBE RAATZE'S CHALLOS

1.8 kg flour

5 cups hot water

2 packets yeast

1/2 cup sugar

1/2 cup oil

2 eggs

2 level tablespoons salt

Prepare as for Egg Challos.

# BREAD, YEAST CAKES, TARTS AND COOKIES

## MEZOINOS ZEMELACH

900 g flour
(white bread flour)

1 3/4 cups hot water

2 packets yeast

1 cup sugar

1 cup oil

2 eggs

1 teaspoon salt

Put the flour in a bowl and make a well in the center. Add the water, yeast and sugar. Mix, then set aside until it starts to froth. Add the other ingredients and knead into a smooth dough. Cover the bowl and allow to rise until doubled in size. Punch down the dough and form into small balls (approximately 25). Lay out on a greased baking tray and let them rise a little. Brush with beaten egg and scatter with a few sesame seeds. Bake in a hot oven at approximately 200°C for 30 minutes.

**TIP:** To give a professional finish, make a short cut with a sharp knife on the top of each ball.

## MEZOINOS CROISSANT WITH ONION

See Mezoinos zemelach for dough and baking instructions.

When the dough has risen, divide it into 6 equal parts. Make a ball of each and roll out into a circle. Spread a little margarine. Chop an onion very finely and sprinkle over the circle, then a little salt and pepper. Cut each circle into four and roll up to form a croissant. Lay out on a greased baking tray, brush with beaten egg and sprinkle with sesame seeds. Let rise again before baking.

## MEZOINOS ZEMELACH WITH RAISINS OR CHOCOLATE CHIPS

See Mezoinos zemelach for dough and baking instructions.

Use 2 cups of water instead of 1 3/4. After adding the oil, eggs and salt also add 200 g raisins or 150 g chocolate chips. Do not sprinkle with sesame seeds.

## CRUMB TOPPING

160 g margarine
150 g powdered sugar
1 teaspoon grated lemon peel
1/2 teaspoon baking powder
175 g flour

Put all the ingredients except the margarine into a bowl. Bring the margarine to a boil and pour immediately over the ingredients. Make a dough. Allow it to cool.
Grate coarsely and use to sprinkle on all kinds of cakes, before baking.

**TIP:** Spread on a baking tray and freeze. Transfer to a closed container in the freezer until needed.

## SURI'S BABKE

**FILLING**

2 eggs

3 cups sugar

1 cup powdered sugar

2 packets vanilla sugar

1 cup cocoa

3 teaspoons instant coffee powder

1 teaspoon cinnamon

200 g margarine

3/4 cup breadcrumbs

Put all ingredients for filling, except the breadcrumbs, in the mixer and whisk well. Add the breadcrumbs and mix a little more. Set aside.

**DOUGH**

1.350 kg flour

3 cups warm water

1 1/2 packets yeast

1 cup sugar

3 egg yolks

200 g margarine

1 level teaspoon salt

1 egg for glazing

Put the flour in a bowl and make a well in the center. Pour in the water, sugar and yeast and leave for five minutes to froth. Add the rest of the ingredients and knead into a dough. Divide the dough into 10 equal parts and roll each one out to a square. Spread the filling over each square and roll up into a long roll. Take two rolls and twist together to form a rope. Lay it lengthwise in a greased 25 cm loaf pan. Continue with the other rolls, making five ropes. Beat an egg with a pinch of salt and sugar and brush over rolls. Leave to rise a little, then bake in a preheated oven at 200°C for 45 minutes.

## KOKOSH CAKE

Use Rogelach dough
(see index)

**FILLING**

5 tablespoons cocoa

12 tablespoons sugar

dried coconut flakes

Divide the dough into 4 equal parts. Roll each out to form a square. Prick with a fork. Brush with oil. Mix together the cocoa and sugar and sprinkle evenly over dough,then sprinkle some dried coconut on top. Roll up and place on a greased baking tray with the ends tucked in underneath. Brush with beaten egg. Bake in a preheated oven at 200°C for approximately 30 minutes.

**TIP:** For a variation, before rolling up the dough, you can scatter some chocolate vermicelli over the filling.

## SHOSHANA'S SHOSHANIM

1 1/2 cups warm water
1 packet yeast
1 kg flour
400 g margarine, in pieces
8 tablespoons sugar
1/2 teaspoon salt
4 eggs

Dissolve the yeast with a little sugar in the water and leave until frothy. Add the rest of the ingredients and make a dough. Allow to rise, then divide into 3 equal parts. Roll out each piece to form a rectangle and brush with oil.

**FILLING**

10 tablespoons sugar
4 tablespoons cocoa
cinnamon

Mix the sugar with the cocoa and spread the mixture over the three pieces of dough. Sprinkle liberally with cinnamon. Roll up each rectangle along its length and cut into 2 cm slices. Place them, cut side down, next to each other in a round baking pan; you will need 3-4 pans. Allow to rise a little before baking. Bake in a preheated oven at 225°C for approximately 30 minutes. Remove from the oven and immediately brush with warmed apricot jam.

**GLAZE**

apricot jam
100 g powdered sugar
2 tablespoons boiling water

Make a glaze with the powdered sugar and boiling water and brush on top of the jam.

## TZOP

**DOUGH**

1 kg flour

1 cup warm water

1 packet yeast

1 cup sugar

375 g margarine at
room temperature

3 eggs

pinch of salt

Put the flour in a bowl and make a well in the center. Pour in the water and add the yeast and sugar. Leave for approximately ten minutes until it starts to froth. Add the rest of the ingredients, mix, and knead to a smooth dough. Cover the bowl with a towel, allow to rise, then leave overnight in the refrigerator.

**FILLING**

200 g margarine

2 cups sugar

4 tablespoons cocoa

cinnamon to taste

**ICING**

100 g powdered sugar

2 tablespoons boiling water

Allow the dough to reach room temperature. Heat ingredients for filling in a pan (do not boil), mixing well. Remove from heat and set aside to thicken.
Divide dough into 6 equal parts. Roll out each one to a thickness of 1/2 cm, spread with filling and fold up like an envelope. Roll out again into a square and cut into 6 equal lengths. Now take two at a time and twist together into a rope. Place the 3 ropes alongside each other in a 22 cm x 14 cm baking tin and bake in a preheated oven at 200°C for half an hour.
Make a glaze with the powdered sugar and boiling water and brush onto warm plaits.

## ROGELACH

**DOUGH**

1 kg flour

2 cups hot water

1 packet yeast

4 tablespoons sugar

400 g margarine

2 egg yolks

pinch of salt

**FILLING**

250 g ground almonds

2 tablespoons brown sugar

2 tablespoons white sugar

1 packet vanilla sugar

2 tablespoons apricot jam

2 tablespoons honey

pinch of cinnamon

grated orange rind (optional)

2 tablespoons raisins (optional)

1 egg white

Put the flour into a bowl and make a well in the center. Pour in the water, yeast and sugar, cover, and leave until frothy. Add the rest of the ingredients and knead into a dough. Cover with a cloth and leave to rise. Meanwhile mix together all the ingredients for the filling. Divide the dough into 8 equal parts and roll out into large circles. Divide each circle into eight equal segments by cutting four evenly-spaced lines through the diameter. Place a spoonful of filling into the center of the widest part of each triangle. Roll them up, starting at the widest end and finishing with the point. Keep the point underneath. Brush with beaten egg. Bake in a preheated oven at approximately 200°C for 25 minutes.

## RAATZE'S ROGELACH

2 cups flour

175 g margarine

1 egg yolk

1 tablespoon sugar

1/2 packet yeast dissolved in 1/4 cup cold water

Make a dough.
Chill in refrigerator for several hours.

**FILLING**

4 tablespoons ground almonds

2 tablespoons sugar

1 packet vanilla sugar

pinch of cinnamon

sugar for rolling

Divide the dough into 4 equal parts. Roll out thinly into circles mix the ingredients for the filling and sprinkle over the 4 circles. Make 6 evenly spaced cuts across the circles creating 12 equal triangles. Roll up each triangle and place on a baking tray. Bake in a preheated oven at 190°C for approximately 25 minutes. Pour some granulated sugar into a bowl and roll the rogelach in the sugar as you take them out of the oven.

**TIP:** These rich and tasty rogelach are highly suitable for special occasions. They freeze well.

## APPLE TART

**DOUGH**

250 g flour

150 g margarine

50 g sugar

pinch of salt

2 egg yolks

3 tablespoons wine

1 packet vanilla sugar

1 teaspoon baking powder

Mix together all the ingredients for the dough. Divide into two parts of 2/3 and 1/3. Roll out the larger piece to line an oiled 20 cm x 30 cm pan.

**FILLING**

matzo meal or ground almonds to sprinkle onto pastry

1 kg cooking apples (Rennet)

2 tablespoons oil

180 g sugar

1 egg for brushing

Peel and grate the apples now (not earlier, so they will not turn brown). Mix the apples with the oil and the sugar. Sprinkle some ground almonds or matzo meal onto the rolled out pastry and spread with the apple mixture. Roll out the second piece of dough and lay it over the apples. Prick all over with a fork. Beat an egg with a little sugar and salt and brush the tart with it. Bake in a preheated oven at 200°C for 45 minutes.

Leave to cool and cut into squares.

## APPLE PIE

**DOUGH**

450 g flour
250 g margarine
1 egg yolk
50 g sugar
1 packet vanilla sugar
1 teaspoon baking powder
pinch of salt
1/2 packet yeast
1/2 cup soda water

Dissolve yeast in soda water.
Combine all ingredients into a dough.
Cover and set aside for half an hour.

**FILLING**

1 kg apples
1 cup sugar
1 cup ground almonds
1 egg for brushing

Peel the apples, cut in quarters and slice thinly. Add sugar. Divide dough in two, roll out one piece and line a 20 cm x 30 cm greased baking pan. Sprinkle 1/2 cup of almonds on the bottom crust, then spread the apples and sprinkle the rest of the almonds on top. Roll out second piece of dough and cover the apple filling with it. Brush with beaten egg.
Bake in preheated oven 225°C for 20 minutes. Lower temperature to 200°C and bake for another 20 minutes.

## ORANGETTES

**DOUGH**

250 g flour

pinch of salt

100 g margarine

60 g sugar

1 packet vanilla sugar

1 egg

1/2 packet baking powder

Combine all ingredients to form a smooth dough and divide into two. Roll out both pieces and use one to line a 20 cm x 30 cm greased baking pan.

**FILLING**

200 g ground almonds

100 g powdered sugar

1 packet vanilla sugar

1/4 cup orange juice

Combine ingredients for filling and spread over the dough. Cover with the second piece of dough. Prick the top layer all over with a fork and then bake in a preheated oven at 180°C for 25 minutes.

**ICING**

100 g powdered sugar

2 tablespoons orange juice

Meanwhile prepare icing by mixing the sifted powdered sugar with the orange juice. Remove the cake from the oven and spread icing over it. Allow to cool, then cut into "fingers."

# CHANUKAH DOUGHNUTS

4 cups flour
1 cup warm water
juice of 1/2 lemon
2 tablespoons oil
1 egg yolk
pinch of salt
3/4 packet yeast
oil for frying
jam
powdered sugar

Put the flour into a bowl, make a well in the center and add the other ingredients in the given order. Knead into a dough. Roll out to approximately 2 cm thickness on a floured board. Cut out circles with the rim of a glass and leave to rise for 1/2 an hour. Fry in a deep fryer on both sides until golden brown. Leave to cool. Slit with a knife and put a teaspoon of jam in the center. Dust with icing sugar before serving.

# HONIG KICHELACH

750 g flour
4 eggs
3/4 cup oil
1 full cup honey
1 1/2 cups sugar
(1/2 a cup of sugar can be replaced with demerara sugar)
2 packets vanilla sugar
1 teaspoon baking soda
1 teaspoon mixed spices
(cinnamon, allspice, nutmeg)

Put the flour into a bowl, make a well in the center and put in all the ingredients. Mix with a mixer, kneading for a few minutes to make a smooth dough. Form into small balls and place on a greased baking tray, leaving room for kichelach to spread. If the dough is sticky, grease hands with a little oil. Bake in a preheated oven at 150°C for 25 minutes.

**TIP:** Keeps well in a closed tin. Need not be frozen. A traditional Rosh Hashana snack.

## HAMANTASHEN

**DOUGH**

250 g flour

pinch of salt

150 g margarine

50 g sugar

1 sachet vanilla sugar

2 egg yolks

3 tablespoons wine

1/2 packet baking powder

**FILLING**

povidel (prune jam)

**GLAZE**

50 g powdered sugar

1 tablespoon boiling water

Combine the ingredients for the dough in the given order. Knead into a dough. If it is sticky, add a little flour. Roll out to approximately 1/2 cm thickness.
Cut out circles of dough with a drinking glass and place a teaspoonful of povidel on each. To form triangles, pinch together two opposite sides towards the center and bring up bottom third to meet it.
Place on a greased baking tray.
Bake in preheated oven at 180°C for 30 minutes until they are light brown.

Mix the powdered sugar with the boiling water and brush the hamantashen with this straight from the oven. Leave to cool.

## EGG KICHELACH

4 eggs
4 teaspoons sugar
1/2 cup oil
2 1/2 cups flour
pinch of salt and pepper

Blend the eggs, sugar and oil together very well. Mix in the flour, salt and pepper and make a dough which is very sticky.

Using plenty of flour, roll out into a square approximately 1 cm thick, and cut into 6 cm squares. Prick the dough with a fork. Arrange kichelach on a baking tray lined with baking parchment and brush them with oil. Bake for 5 minutes in a preheated oven at 250°C, then turn heat down to 200°C and bake for another 15 minutes or so.

**TIP:** The pastry should not be rolled more than once. Freezes well.

# BREAD, YEAST CAKES, TARTS AND COOKIES

## CHOCOLATE BALLS

400 g crushed plain biscuits

200 g margarine

18 tablespoons sugar

10 tablespoons cocoa

cinnamon to taste

14 tablespoons water
(may substitute wine for part)

1 packet vanilla sugar

dried coconut or
ground almonds for decoration

Mix the sugar, cocoa and water together and boil until the sugar has dissolved. (Mix some wine with the water for a more sophisticated taste.) Add the margarine and allow to melt. Remove from the heat. Add the crushed biscuits and mix together well. Chill in the refrigerator until set, and then form into balls. Roll the balls in dried coconut or ground almonds. Store in a cool place.

**TIP:** For special occasions, dip the balls in beaten egg white and then roll in chocolate vermicelli.

## SESAME SNACK

1 tablespoon honey

1/3 cup sugar

2 cups sesame seeds

Melt the sugar and honey over a low flame (2 to 3 minutes). Add the sesame seeds and stir for 10 minutes. Roll out the mixture to a thickness of 1 cm with a greased rolling pin on a pastry board. Cut into squares while warm.

## ROSETTES

300 g flour

200 g margarine

2 egg yolks

1/2 packet fresh yeast crumbled and mixed with 2 tablespoons sugar

pinch of salt

1 tablespoon rum

Mix ingredients together to make a dough and place in freezer for 1/2 hour to firm. Roll out to a square 1/2 cm thick.

**FILLING**

2 egg whites

70 g sugar

1 packet vanilla sugar

Whisk egg whites until stiff, add sugar and vanilla sugar. Spread the egg white over the pastry, roll up and cut into slices 1/2 cm thick. Place slices with their cut side down on a greased baking tray and bake for 30 minutes in preheated oven at 170°C.

## REFRIGERATOR COOKIES (THREE VERSIONS)

250 g margarine
(at room temperature)

150 g powdered sugar

2 packets vanilla sugar

2 egg whites

400 g flour

pinch of salt

Mix the margarine with the sugar and vanilla sugar, then add the egg whites one at a time and the salt, mixing continuously. Add the flour last and knead into a dough. Chill in refrigerator for an hour.

COOKIE NO. 1
Divide dough in half. Roll out one half thinly and cut into circles.Repeat with the second half but cut small circles out of the center of these circles. Bake* at 180°C and leave to cool. Stick together in two's with red jam, using one plain cookie and one with a hole on top.

COOKIE NO. 2
Cut into circles. Bake* at 180°C. Stick together with your favourite chocolate spread, and if desired dip halfway in melted chocolate.

COOKIE NO. 3
Cut into desired shape, brush with beaten egg and sprinkle with almond flakes, then bake* at 180°C.

*These cookies should be baked for approximately 25 minutes.

# Notes

# A L L  K I N D S  O F  C A K E S

Birthday cake
Mocha cream frosting
Belgian marzipan speciality
Zerbo layer cake
Almond fluden
Domino layer cake
Extra light coconut cake
Coconut cake
Tante Tzippi's light orange cake
Nechama's orange cake
Fluffy cupcakes
Hazelnut freezer cake
My sister's sponge lekach
Swiss roll
Apple roll
Strawberry cream cake
Oma's honey cake
My sister's honey cake
Gingerbread
Purim fluden
Simple chocolate cake
Quick chocolate cake
Chocolate cake
Chocolate sponge cake
Chocolate vermicelli cake
Special chocolate cake
Mocha cake
Mirel's cake
Special brownies

# BIRTHDAY CAKE

5 eggs
150 g sugar
150 g flour
1/2 teaspoon baking powder
150 g finely ground almonds
few drops almond essence

Beat the eggs with the sugar until fairly stiff. Mix the flour with the baking powder and fold into the eggs with a spatula; then add the almonds. Pour into a greased 22 cm round cake pan.
Bake for 45 minutes at 175°C.

**SYRUP**

150 g sugar
1/2 cup water
1/4 cup of cognac
powdered sugar for dusting

Prepare the syrup by boiling the water and sugar on a high flame for ten minutes. Remove from the heat and stir in the cognac. When the cake has baked for 45 minutes remove from the oven and carefully pour the syrup all over the cake. Return to the oven for a further 15 minutes. When baked, leave to cool slightly and then carefully remove from pan. Dust with powdered sugar before serving.

**TIP:** Use a baking pan with a loose bottom for easier removal.

**OPTIONAL CHOCOLATE TOPPING**

150 g chocolate
25 g margarine
2 tablespoons water

Melt the chocolate. Cut the margarine into pieces and add, together with the water. Blend until smooth, spread over cake and leave to set.

## MOCHA CREAM FROSTING

400 g margarine

1/2 kg powdered sugar

3 packets vanilla sugar

4 teaspoons instant coffee powder
+ 2 teaspoons boiling water

1 large egg

a few drops of rum

Cream the margarine with the sugar with a mixer. Add the vanilla sugar and mix for 10 minutes. Dissolve the coffee powder in boiling water, add stir into the mixture. Add egg yolk first, then the egg white if necessary and mix well. Keeps for a long time in a closed container in the refrigerator.

Good for Swiss rolls, and filling or decorating cakes.

# BELGIAN MARZIPAN SPECIALITY

250 g margarine

330 g soft brown sugar

1/2 cup orange juice

1/2 kg flour

2 teaspoons mixed spices
(cinnamon, allspice, nutmeg)

1 teaspoon baking soda

pinch of salt

Mix the margarine with the sugar, add the juice, then the rest of the ingredients and knead into a dough.Chill for one hour in refrigerator. Divide the pastry into two and roll out into a square 1 cm thick.
Line a large baking tray with baking parchment and place half the dough on it (the pastry need not cover the whole tray).

**FILLING**

600 g marzipan

water or egg white

powdered sugar for rolling out

Add a little water or egg white to the marzipan to make it easier to roll out. Sprinkle powdered sugar on the board and roll it out to a thickness of 1 cm. Lay this filling on the pastry. Cover the marzipan with the second sheet of pastry and brush with beaten egg. Bake slowly in a preheated oven at approximately 170°C for 50 minutes. Leave to cool. Cut into slices.

## ZERBO LAYER CAKE

**DOUGH**

450 g flour

250 g margarine

3 egg yolks

1/2 cup water

2 tablespoons sugar

pinch of salt

1 packet baking powder

Mix the margarine into the flour, add the rest of the ingredients and mix into a dough. Divide into three parts.

**FILLING**

450 g finely ground walnuts

150 g powdered sugar

2 packets vanilla sugar

grated rind of 1 lemon

2 tablespoons lemon juice

1 egg white

apricot jam for spreading

Mix together all ingredients for the filling very well. Roll out one piece of dough and use to line a 20 cm x 30 cm greased baking pan. Spread with apricot jam and cover with half the filling. Roll out the second piece of dough, place on top and spread with jam and the rest of the filling. Roll out last piece of dough and place on top. Prick all over with a fork and bake in a preheated oven at 180°C for 40 minutes.

**TOPPING**

150 g chocolate

20 g margarine

Melt the chocolate with the margarine. Spread over cake and leave to cool, then cut into squares.

This cake is a Hungarian speciality.

## ALMOND FLUDEN

*Use Apple tart dough*
*(see p. 140)*

**WHITE PART**

1/2 kg peeled ground almonds

350 g sugar

4 egg whites

juice of 1 lemon

**DARK PART**

1/2 kg unpeeled ground almonds

350 g sugar

4 egg whites

juice of 1 lemon

2 tablespoons cocoa

apricot jam for spreading

Mix together in separate bowls the ingredients of each part. Line a 20 cm x 30 cm greased baking tray with the pastry. Spread first with the white nut mixture, then spread with some apricot jam and finally top with the dark mixture. Bake in preheated oven at aproximately 180°C for 1 hour, until golden. Leave to cool overnight and cut into small squares.

This is an old Polish recipe.

# DOMINO LAYER CAKE

**DARK LAYER**

7 eggs, separated

1 cup sugar

2 packets vanilla sugar

200 g margarine

2 cups ground almonds

1 tablespoon cocoa

5 tablespoons flour

1 teaspoon baking powder

Cream the margarine with half the sugar and vanilla sugar. Slowly add the egg yolks. Mix the cocoa with the almonds and fold into the mixture with the flour, using a spatula. Whisk the egg whites until stiff, add the rest of the sugar, and fold into the mixture with spatula. Line a 25 cm x 35 cm baking tin with baking parchment and pour in the mixture. Bake in a preheated oven at 180°C for 25 minutes.

**LIGHT LAYER**

7 eggs, separated

1 cup sugar

2 packets vanilla sugar

200 g margarine

juice and rind of half a lemon

10 tablespoons flour

1 teaspoon baking powder

Follow the instructions for cake 1, and bake.

**CREAM**

1 egg +1 yolk

1 cup sugar

150 g margarine at room temperature

200 g chocolate

1/4 cup water

Beat the eggs with the margarine and half a cup of sugar. Heat the chocolate with the other half cup of sugar and water on a low flame. Blend slowly with the egg mixture. Spread half the cream on the baked dark cake. Place the lighter cake on top and spread with the rest of the cream. Leave to set, cut into squares and serve in individual cake papers.

Freezes well.

# EXTRA LIGHT COCONUT CAKE

**BASE**

10 egg yolks

10 tablespoons sugar

1 packet vanilla sugar

10 tablespoons oil

5 tablespoons cognac

5 tablespoons water

16 tablespoons flour

1 teaspoon baking powder

Whisk the egg yolks with the sugars until stiff. Slowly add the rest of the ingredients, folding the flour in with a spatula. Pour into a large, greased 25 cm x 35 cm pan.

**TOPPING**

150 g grated chocolate

10 egg whites

1 3/4 cups sugar

2 cups dried coconut

Sprinkle the grated chocolate over the mixture in the pan. Whisk the egg whites until stiff, then slowly add the sugar. Fold the coconut in with a spatula and spread over the cake mixture. Bake in a preheated oven at 180°C for 35 to 45 minutes.
Allow to cool.
Cut into squares.

## COCONUT CAKE

6 egg yolks
150 g sugar
300 g margarine
4 1/2 cups flour
1/2 packet baking powder
5 tablespoons jam
5 tablespoons cocoa

**TOPPING**
8 egg whites
1 1/2 cups sugar
250 g dried coconut
juice of 1/2 lemon

Mix egg yolks, sugar, margarine, flour and baking powder into a dough. Divide into two. Roll out one part and use to line a greased 25 cm x 35 cm baking pan. Mix the cocoa and jam into the second half of the dough. Roll out and place on top of the first piece of dough. Bake in a preheated oven at 180°C for 25 minutes.

Meanwhile whisk 8 egg whites until stiff and slowly add 1 1/2 cups of sugar. Fold in the lemon juice and the dried coconut. Remove the cake from the oven and spread the topping. Bake for another half hour. When cold cut into squares.

## TANTE TZIPPI'S LIGHT ORANGE CAKE

4 eggs, separated
1 cup sugar
1/2 cup oil
3/4 cup orange juice
2 1/2 cups flour
1 teaspoon baking powder

Whisk the egg whites until stiff. Slowly add the sugar, egg yolks, oil and juice, whisking all the time. Fold in the flour and baking powder with a spatula. Bake in a loaf pan in a preheated oven at 180°C for approximately 45 minutes.

## NECHAMA'S ORANGE CAKE

6 eggs, separated
2 1/4 cups  sugar
5 packets vanilla sugar
200 g margarine
1 cup freshly squeezed orange juice
4 1/2 cups flour
1 packet baking powder
1 tablespoon each of cocoa, sugar, water for contrast

Beat the egg yolks with half the sugar, add the margarine in pieces and mix well. Add the orange juice, flour and baking powder and mix. Whisk the egg whites with the rest of the sugar and vanilla sugar until stiff. Fold this into the first mixture with a spatula. Pour the batter into two greased rectangular cake pans, leaving a little in the bowl. Mix together cocoa, sugar and water. Add to the remaining batter and spread over the surface of the two cakes. Bake in a preheated oven at 170°C for an hour.
Remove from the oven and allow to cool.

## FLUFFY CUPCAKES

200 g margarine
350 g sugar
3 packets vanilla sugar
5 eggs
3/4 cup orange juice
450 g flour
1 packet baking powder

Cream the margarine with the sugars with a mixer until light and fluffy. Add the eggs one at a time, mixing well after each addition. Add the orange juice and mix well. Finally fold in the flour and baking powder. Fill paper cupcake tin liners 3/4 full with the batter.
Bake in a preheated oven at 160°C for 30 minutes.

Can be decorated. Cupcakes are a perfect snack to take to school or on trips.

# HAZELNUT FREEZER CAKE

**PART I**

12 egg whites

1 cup sugar

300 g ground roasted hazelnuts

Whisk the egg whites until very stiff. Add the sugar slowly and fold in the ground nuts carefully with a spatula. Pour into a 25 cm x 35 cm greased baking pan and bake in a pre-heated oven at 180°C for 25 minutes.

**PART II**

12 egg yolks

1/2 cup sugar

3 packets vanilla sugar

200 g margarine at room temperature

200 g chocolate

1/2 cup water

While the cake is baking, cream the margarine with the sugar. Slowly add the egg yolks. Melt the chocolate with the water over a low flame and slowly add to the margarine and sugar mixture. Remove the cake from the oven and pour the mixture over it. Return to the oven and bake for another 30 minutes. Allow to cool, cut into squares and keep frozen.

**TIP:** Moisten the knife to cut smoothly.

## MY SISTER'S SPONGE LEKACH

**PART I**

6 tablespoons sugar

4 tablespoons cocoa

pinch of cinnamon

6 tablespoons water

200 g margarine
at room temperature

Heat the sugar, cocoa and cinnamon together gently in a pan. Cut the margarine into small pieces and add, stirring until it has melted (do not boil). Set aside.

**PART II**

12 eggs, separated

340 g sugar

4 cups flour

1 packet baking powder

Whisk the egg whites until very stiff. Slowly add the sugar, then add the egg yolks one at a time, mixing well after each addition. Fold in the flour and baking powder with a spatula. Mix a third of the batter together with the chocolate cream. Line a 25 cm x 35 cm baking pan with greaseproof paper. Pour the two mixtures into the pan in alternate layers, starting with the light mixture, continuing with a thinner layer of the dark, and repeating, ending with the light mixture on top. Bake in a preheated oven at 180°C for approximately 1 hour.

This cake is perfect for special occasions and freezes very well. For a smaller lekach, make half the amount.

*Birthday cake*
*Rogelach*
*Apple tart*
*Chocolate vermicelli cake*
*Honey cake*
*Fluffy cupcakes*

## SWISS ROLL

5 eggs, separated

140 g sugar

70 g finely ground almonds

a few drops of almond essence

25 g sliced almonds

Whisk the egg yolks with the sugar. Fold in the ground almonds with a spatula. Whisk the egg whites until very stiff and fold into the mixture. Line a 25 cm x 35 cm greased baking pan and pour in the mixture. Sprinkle with the almonds and bake in a preheated oven at 180°C for 20 to 25 minutes.

Sprinkle flour over a tea towel, remove the cake from the oven, allow to cool slightly, then turn the cake out onto the towel. Remove the paper and roll up the cake. Unroll and fill when entirely cold.

**FILLING**
(make just before use)

250 g whipping cream

1 teaspoon sugar

strawberries

powdered sugar for dusting

Whip the cream with the sugar. Take a few strawberries, wash, hull and slice finely. Spread the unrolled cake with cream, arrange the strawberries on top, and then roll it back up. Dust with powdered sugar. Keep refrigerated.

## APPLE ROLL

4 eggs

5 tablespoons sugar

1 packet vanilla sugar

5 tablespoons flour

pinch of baking powder

pinch of cinnamon

**FILLING**

2 1/2 sweet apples
(Golden Delicious)

1 tablespoon sugar

2 tablespoons white raisins

Whisk the eggs with all the sugars until stiff. Fold in the flour, cinnamon and baking powder with a spatula. Line a large baking pan, 30 cm x 40 cm, with baking parchment. Grease and sprinkle with another tablespoon of sugar.

Peel and grate the apples and spread around the pan, then sprinkle raisins on top. Now pour the batter over the apples and raisins and bake in a preheated oven at 175°C for 20 minutes.

Lay out a dish towel and dust with powdered sugar, remove the cake and turn it out face down onto the towel. Carefully remove the paper then roll up the cake, leaving the free end underneath.

Cover with the towel and leave to cool.

## STRAWBERRY CREAM CAKE

3 eggs, separated
1 1/2 cups sugar
1/4 cup oil
1/2 cup soda water
1 tablespoon lemon juice
250 g flour
2 teaspoons baking powder

**FILLING AND TOPPING**

500 g whipping cream
1 tablespoon powdered sugar
500 g strawberries

Whisk the egg whites until stiff. Slowly, while whisking, add sugar, egg yolks, oil, water and lemon juice. Add the flour and baking powder with a spatula. Pour into a greased 25 cm round baking pan and bake for 40 minutes in a preheated oven at 180°C. Remove and cool.

Mix whipping cream or parve whip with powdered sugar. Cut the cake in half horizontally. Spread the bottom half with cream and arrange strawberries on top. Cover with the other half of the the cake and top with cream and fruit.

**TIP:** You can also freeze the cake whole and when you need it, defrost it, cut it through and fill it before serving.

# ALL KINDS OF CAKES

## OMA'S HONEY CAKE

2 eggs
225 g sugar
1/2 cup oil
250 g clear honey
1 cup dark beer
1/2 kg flour
1 teaspoon baking soda

Whisk the eggs with the sugar until stiff. While mixing slowly add the oil, honey and beer. Finally add the flour and baking soda. Pour into two greased 25 cm loaf pans and bake in a preheated oven at 175°C for approximately half an hour.
Reduce temperature to 160°C to prevent burning and bake for a further half hour.

## MY SISTER'S HONEY CAKE

6 eggs, separated
1 cup granulated sugar
1/2 cup demerara sugar
1/2 cup oil
1/2 kg clear honey
1 cup of water
1 tablespoon dissolved instant coffee
5 1/2 cups flour
1 1/2 teaspoons baking soda
1 1/2 teaspoons baking powder
1 teaspoon mixed spices (cinnamon, nutmeg, allspice)

Whisk the egg yolks with the brown sugar until stiff. While mixing, add the oil, honey, water, coffee and flour with the baking powder, baking soda and spices. Whisk the egg whites in separate bowl, slowly add sugar and beat until stiff. Fold this carefully into the first mixture with a spatula. Pour into a greased 25 cm x 35 cm baking pan and bake in a preheated oven at 160°C for approximately 1 hour.

This is an exceptionally light honey cake.

## GINGERBREAD

7 eggs, separated

2 cups sugar

1/2 cup oil

3/4 cup honey

1/2 cup water, mixed
with 1/2 cup wine

3 1/2 cups flour

1 teaspoon baking powder

1 teaspoon baking soda

2 teaspoons cocoa

3 teaspoons mixed spices
(cinnamon, allspice, nutmeg)

Whisk the egg yolks with 1 cup of sugar until fluffy. While mixing, add the oil, honey, wine and water mixture, and then the dry ingredients. Whisk the egg whites, slowly adding the second cup of sugar, until stiff. Fold carefully into the first mixture with a spatula. Bake in two or three greased loaf pans in a preheated oven at 160-170°C for approximately an hour.

# PURIM FLUDEN

**DOUGH**

350 g flour

pinch of salt

200 g margarine

100 g sugar

1 egg + 1 egg yolk

2 tablespoons cold water

1/2 packet baking powder

Mix all the ingredients into a dough and divide into three parts, with one piece slightly larger than the other two.

**FIRST FILLING**

apricot jam

100 g ground walnuts

100 g chopped dates

2 tablespoons orange juice

1/2 teaspoon cinnamon

**SECOND FILLING**

apricot jam

450 g sour cooking apples (Rennet), grated

70 g sugar

**TOPPING**

1 egg white

1 packet vanilla sugar

Mix together ingredients for first filling well. Roll out the largest piece of dough and use to line a greased 20 cm x 30 cm baking pan. Spread with two tablespoons of apricot jam, and cover the dough with the first filling. Roll out another piece of dough, place it on top, and spread with jam. Mix together the ingredients of the second filling and spread it. Roll out the third piece of dough and place it on top. Bake in a preheated oven at 200°C for 40 minutes. Whisk the egg white until stiff and add the vanilla sugar.

Remove the fluden from the oven and top with the egg white. Return to the oven, reduce the temperature a little, and bake for a further 20 minutes. Allow to cool and cut into squares.

## SIMPLE CHOCOLATE CAKE

1 cup boiling water

5 tablespoons cocoa

50 g melted margarine

3 eggs

1 1/2 cups sugar

2 packets vanilla sugar

2 1/2 cups flour

1 teaspoon baking powder

Mix the water with the cocoa and the margarine. Whisk the egg whites until stiff and add the sugar, then the egg yolks and the cooled chocolate mixture. Add the flour and baking powder. Pour into a greased loaf pan and bake for 50 minutes in a preheated oven at 180°C.

## QUICK CHOCOLATE CAKE

6 eggs

750 g sugar

2 packets vanilla sugar

6 tablespoons cocoa

2 cups oil

2 cups Coca Cola

750 g flour

1 packet baking powder

Put all ingredients except the flour and baking powder into the mixer and mix well. Mix in the flour and baking powder. Pour batter into a greased 25 cm x 35 cm baking pan and bake for 1 hour 20 minutes in a preheated oven at 180°C.

## CHOCOLATE CAKE

1/2 cup water
1 cup sugar
4 tablespoons cocoa
200 g margarine

Mix the water, sugar and cocoa and bring to a boil. Add the margarine in small pieces and allow to melt. Set aside to cool.

6 eggs, separated
1 cup sugar
2 cups flour
1 teaspoon baking powder

Mix egg yolks, one at a time, into chocolate mixture. Add the flour and baking powder. Whisk the egg whites until stiff and slowly add the sugar, then fold into the chocolate mixture. Pour into a 25 cm x 35 cm greased baking pan and bake in a preheated oven at 180°C for 1 hour. Dust with powdered sugar, and cut into squares.

## CHOCOLATE SPONGE CAKE

200 g sugar
100 g margarine
3 eggs
100 g finely ground almonds
50 g cocoa
pinch of cinnamon
150 g flour
1 teaspoon baking powder

Cream the sugar and the margarine. Add the eggs one at a time while mixing. Fold in the dry ingredients with a spatula. Bake in a greased loaf pan for 50 minutes in a preheated oven at 180°C.

## CHOCOLATE VERMICELLI CAKE

10 eggs

2 cups sugar

1/2 cup oil

1/4 cup fresh orange or lemon juice

200 g chocolate vermicelli

3 cups flour

1/2 packet baking powder

Whisk the eggs with the sugar until stiff. Slowly add the oil and the juice. Fold in the vermicelli, flour and baking powder with a spatula. Pour into a large tin and bake for approximately 50 minutes in a preheated oven at 180°C.

## SPECIAL CHOCOLATE CAKE

200 g sugar

100 g margarine

3 eggs

1/4 cup soda water

100 g ground almonds

1 tablespoon cocoa

a few drops of rum

pinch of cinnamon

150 g flour

1/2 teaspoon baking powder

Cream the sugar with the margarine. Add the eggs one at a time mixing after each one. Add the water. Mix alternate spoonfuls of almonds, flour and cocoa into batter with a spatula. Add the rest of the ingredients and spoon into a greased rectangular baking pan. Bake in a preheated oven at 170°C for approximately 50 minutes.

## MOCHA CAKE

6 eggs, separated

2 cups sugar

1/2 cup oil

3/4 cup boiling water

3 teaspoons instant coffee powder

1 cup ground almonds

2 cups flour + 1 teaspoon baking powder

Dissolve the coffee in the boiling water, and cool. Whisk the egg whites until stiff. Slowly add the sugar and egg yolks, then the coffee and the oil. Fold in the flour and the almonds with a spatula. Pour into a 25 cm x 35 cm greased baking pan and bake in a preheated oven at 180°C for 1 hour. Allow to cool before turning out.

## MIREL'S CAKE

10 eggs

350 g sugar

1 packet vanilla sugar

1 cup oil

1/2 cup soda water

200 g chocolate vermicelli

100 g ground almonds

pinch of cinnamon

4 cups flour

2 teaspoons baking powder

Whisk the eggs with the sugars until stiff. Add the oil and the water. Fold in the flour and baking powder, vermicelli and almonds with a spatula. Bake in a 25 cm x 35 cm greased baking pan in a preheated oven at 180°C for 1 hour.

## SPECIAL BROWNIES

3 full tablespoons creamy
peanut butter

100 g margarine

1 1/2 cups light
brown sugar

1 packet vanilla sugar

3 eggs

pinch of salt

2 1/2 cups flour

1 teaspoon baking powder

100 g baking chocolate

Cream the margarine, peanut butter and sugars in the mixer. Add the eggs one at a time, mixing after each one. Finally add the flour, salt and baking powder. Melt the chocolate in a double boiler. Pour one third of the batter into a separate bowl and mix in the chocolate. Pour half of the light batter into a 20 cm x 30 cm greased baking pan. Drop large spoonfuls of the dark mixture into the pan, then fill the rest of the area with spoonfuls of the remaining light mixture. Bake in a preheated oven at 160°C for 30 minutes. Cut into squares when cool.

# Notes

# TRADITIONAL SHABBOS & YOM TOV

Shabbos soup

Soup nockerlach

Cholent

Mehl kugel

Galerette

Bubbe Raatze's kugel

Potato kugel

Yerushalmi kugel

Sweet lokshen kugel

Pashtida (two-color)

Brayne's apple kugel

Apple kugel

Mayeren (carrot) tzimmes

Carrot and prune tzimmes

Kreplach

Potato latkes

## SHABBOS SOUP

2 1/2 kg chicken giblets
1 turkey wing or 1/4 boiler
5 medium leeks
1/2 celery root
1 parsnip
6 carrots
2 zucchini
1 piece of pumpkin
2 turnips
1 onion
2 cloves garlic
1 small fennel
10 cups water

Rinse the giblets and poultry well. Put into a pot with the water, and bring to a boil. Skim. Peel all the vegetables, cut them into pieces, and put into the pot. Cover and simmer for 4 hours (or 1 hour 15 minutes in a pressure cooker). Strain the soup when cold.

**TIP:** Serve with soup nockerlach.

## SOUP NOCKERLACH

*(for 4 people)*
1 large egg
pinch of salt and pepper
2 tablespoons oil
25 g matzo meal

Mix egg, salt, pepper and oil. Add matzo meal. Set aside for a few hours (or overnight) in refrigerator. Prepare a cup of boiling water. Dip a teaspoon into the hot water and then take a spoonful of the mixture and drop into boiling soup, and repeat. Cook for 2 to 3 minutes.

**TIP:** Delicious with Shabbos soup.

# TRADITIONAL SHABBOS & YOMTOV

## CHOLENT

1 1/2 cups white beans

1/2 cup light brown beans

1 onion

1 clove garlic

one turkey thigh (or similar meat)

4 potatoes

paprika

oil

salt

sugar

Soak the beans in cold water overnight. Drain. Put the beans in a pan of cold water and bring to a boil. Drain and repeat. Pour into a colander and rinse well with cold water. Check the beans for worms. Put a tablespoon of sugar in a pan with a little oil and caramelize. Add the beans and shake well over a low flame. Add salt, sliced onion, garlic, 2 cups of hot water and the turkey (cut into two if large). Cover and cook for an hour. Peel the potatoes, cut into small pieces, sprinkle with paprika and add. Add 1 cup boiling water. Cook for a further half hour. Before Shabbos, bring to a boil and place on a Shabbos hotplate without adding water.

## MEHL KUGEL

1/2 cup sunflower oil

1/2 cup water

1 teaspoon paprika

1 teaspoon soup powder

2 cups flour

Mix all ingredients together to form a dough, form into a large dumpling and add to the cholent.

**TIP:** The mixture can also be used to stuff a helzel (chicken neck skin).

*Carrot & prune tzimmes*
*Cholent*
*Shabbos soup*
*Galerette*
*Yerushalmi kugel*

## GALERETTE

1 veal shin-bone, cut in pieces

1 beef shin-bone, cut in pieces

2 whole heads of garlic

12 cups water

paprika

pepper, salt

Pour boiling water over the bones and rinse well. Put into a large pot with the water and the peeled garlic. Cover, bring to a boil, skim, and cook for 6 hours. During the last hour, add 2 teaspoons paprika, 1 teaspoon black pepper and two teaspoons salt. Remove from heat and leave to cool slightly. Remove the bones from the pot and trim off the meat. Cut it into small pieces and return these to the pot and cook for a while. Pour into a large tray and leave to cool completely. Leave to set overnight in the refrigerator. Remove the layer of fat that forms on top. Cut into squares before serving.

**TIP:** Can be frozen but must then be boiled up and left to set again.

# BUBBE RAATZE'S KUGEL

200 g challah dough
oil
apricot jam

Put the challah dough into a soup plate and cover with another deep soup plate. Leave until it has risen fully (at least an hour). Then knead briefly and roll out very thin on a floured surface. Brush first with oil, and then spread apricot jam.

**FILLING**

I Golden Delicious apple, peeled and chopped

2 tablespoons brown sugar

2 tablespoons white sugar

3 tablespoons ground almonds

pinch of cinnamon

1 handful raisins

Mix all the filling ingredients and spread on the dough. Roll up, then twist around in a coil. Fry on both sides in a little oil in a small covered saucepan.
My Bubbe Raatze always served small pieces of this on Friday night.

Can be served hot or cold.

## POTATO KUGEL
## (ALSO FOR PESACH)

5 kg potatoes

6 eggs

1 cup oil

5 level teaspoons salt

pepper to taste

1 minced onion (optional)

3 tablespoons matzo meal
(optional)

Grate the potatoes coarsely (if there is a lot of liquid, discard it). Mix all ingredients together. Pour into a greased 25 cm x 35 cm baking dish and bake in a preheated oven at 225°C for half an hour. Reduce to 200°C and bake for another 1 1/2 hours. If you think it is getting too brown, cover with a piece of aluminum foil. The kugel tastes even better if you add an extra 1/2 cup of oil, but of course this also greatly increases the fat content.

**TIP:** You can wrap a piece of kugel in aluminum foil or greaseproof paper and put it in the cholent.

# YERUSHALMI KUGEL

1 kg medium width noodles
1 cup oil
1 cup sugar
11 cups water
10 tablespoons sugar
4 teaspoons salt
1 teaspoon black pepper
6 large eggs

Caramelize 1 cup of sugar in the oil in a large pot. Remove from the heat and, taking extreme care as the melted sugar is very hot and likely to splash, add the water, one cup at a time, covering the pot after each addition. Add the rest of the sugar, salt and pepper and bring back to a boil. Add the noodles to the pot, and cook for two minutes, then remove from the flame. Leave covered until all the water is absorbed. Mix in the eggs and pour into a greased baking dish of 25 cm x 35 cm. Bake in a preheated oven at 200°C for approximately 1 hour 30 minutes. If the kugel becomes too brown, cover with aluminum foil.

**TIP:** Freezes well. Also delicious wrapped in aluminum foil and kept warm in the cholent.

## SWEET LOKSHEN KUGEL

750 g wide noodles
250 g fine noodles
10 tablespoons sugar
3 tablespoons brown sugar
4 packets vanilla sugar
100 g white raisins
100 g glacé cherries
200 g ground almonds
cinnamon to taste
grated rind of 1/2 lemon
2 sour apples (Granny Smith) diced finely
8 eggs

Cook the noodles in lightly salted water and drain. Mix the noodles with all the ingredients except the eggs. Then add the eggs, mixing well. Bake in a deep greased pan of 30 cm x 25 cm at 200°C for 1 3/4 hours. If it gets too brown, cover with aluminium foil.

Freezes well.

## PASHTIDA (TWO-COLOR)

1 kg potatoes

1 kg sweet potatoes plus
1/2 kg peeled potatoes

3 eggs

4 tablespoons oil

salt and pepper

Boil 1 kg peeled potatoes in lightly salted water. Drain and return to flame to dry out for a moment. Mash. Peel and prepare the sweet potatoes together with the 1/2 kg ordinary potatoes in the same way, and place in a separate bowl. To the first mixture add two eggs, two tablespoons oil, salt and pepper to taste. To the second batch add one egg, two tablespoons oil, salt and pepper.

Divide the first mashed potato mixture between two greased 25 cm rectangular baking pans. Cover with the sweet potato mixture. Bake in a preheated oven at 200°C for 1 hour 10 minutes.

Make sure not to overbake.

## BRAYNE'S APPLE KUGEL

4 eggs

1 cup sugar

2 packets vanilla sugar

1/2 cup oil

2 cups flour

1 teaspoon baking powder

cinnamon to taste

500 g sweet cooking apples (JonaGold)

Whisk the eggs and sugars until stiff. Slowly add the oil, flour, baking powder and cinnamon. Peel and core the apples, cut into small pieces and fold into mixture. Pour into a 20 cm x 30 cm greased baking pan.

Bake in a preheated oven at 190°C for 45 minutes.

Can be served hot or cold.

## APPLE KUGEL

5 eggs

1 1/2 cups sugar

1/2 cup oil

2 cups flour

1 level teaspoon baking soda

1 cup raisins

1 cup ground almonds

1/2 teaspoon cinnamon (optional)

750 g grated cooking apples (Rennet)

Whisk the eggs with the sugar until stiff. Add the other ingredients in the given order. Pour into a greased 20 cm x 30 cm baking pan and bake in a preheated oven at 200°C for 1 hour.

Can be served hot or cold.

## MAYEREN (CARROT) TZIMMES

1/2 kg carrots
3 tablespoons oil
1 level tablespoon sugar
1 tablespoon honey
1/4 teaspoon salt

Peel and slice the carrots. Put into a pan with 3 tablespoons oil. Sauté for 15 minutes, stirring occasionally. Remove from the heat, add the sugar, salt and honey and simmer for another 15 minutes. Serve hot.

## CARROT AND PRUNE TZIMMES

750 g carrots
20 g margarine
1/2 cup water
15 pitted prunes
100 g blanched almonds
1 tablespoon sugar
1 tablespoon honey
pinch of salt

Soak the prunes in water for two hours. Peel and slice the carrots. Put in a pan with the water and margarine. Cover and simmer for 15 minutes. Add the sugar, honey and salt. Drain the prunes and add together with the almonds. Cover and simmer for a further 1/2 hour, shaking the pan occasionally to prevent burning. Serve hot with meat.

## KREPLACH

For the pastry and cooking method
see Pirogen.

**FILLING**

200 g ground beef
200 g ground veal
1 onion
1 small egg
2 tablespoons matzo meal
a little pepper

Chop the onion finely and brown in a pan
with a little oil. Mix in all the ingredients.
Roll the pastry out thinly and cut into
squares of approximately 8 cm. Put a teaspoon of filling on each square and fold
over into a triangle.

**TIP:** When freezing, freeze on a tray first,
then pack in boxes or bags, to prevent
them sticking together.

## POTATO LATKES

1/2 kg potatoes
1 egg
salt and pepper to taste
oil

Peel and finely grate the potatoes.
Add the egg, salt and pepper and mix well.
Heat a frying pan with a little oil. Drop in spoonfuls of the mixture and fry on both sides until golden brown. Serve hot.

**TIP:** Make up your mixture with 1/2 kg potatoes at a time, even when making larger quantities, to avoid the mixture discoloring.
A typical Jewish delicacy which is served on Chanukah and festive occasions.

# Notes

# P E S A C H

Opa's charoises

Pesach gefilte fish

Mock fish (falshe fish)

Pesachdige egg with onion

Cream of vegetable soup

Oma's bubbelach

Chicken kneidlach

Matzo meal kneidlach

Pesach noodles

Borsht

Mayonnaise

Matzo torte

Zucchini

Carrot tzimmes

Pesach cholent

Goulash

Meat patties

Pesachdige schnitzel

Chicken à l'orange

Chicken in wine

Chicken in the oven

Carrot kugel

Auntie Aidel's apple jam

Apple kugel

Orange squash concentrate

Apple blintzes

Hearty potato blintzes

Matzo meal torte

Almond tart

Pesach chocolate cake I

Pesach chocolate cake II

Potato-starch cake

Almond and potato-starch cake

Coconut flavored cake

Fluden

Malka's marzipan balls

Oma Ollech's almond macaroons

Almond cookies

Coconut cookies

Chocolate spread

## OPA'S CHAROISES

1 Golden Delicious apple

3/4 cup walnuts

1 level teaspoon ginger

1 level teaspoon cinnamon

3 tablespoons red wine

Peel and core the apple and chop finely. Chop the nuts and add to the apple with the spices. Mix in the wine just before serving.

Charoises is used at the Seder table. Cover with cling film and keep refrigerated.

## PESACH GEFILTE FISH

**FISH MIXTURE**

1 1/2 kg ground carp

1 1/2 kg ground salmon trout

6 tablespoons minced onion

5 eggs

225 g ground almonds

300 g sugar

6 level teaspoons salt

pepper to taste

**STOCK**
(fish yoch)
*amount for each
kg of fish:*

4 cups water

4 tablespoons sugar

1/2 teaspoon salt

pinch of pepper

1 chopped onion

2 carrots

Mix all ingredients together well by hand or with a mixer. Take 6 sheets of greaseproof paper (30 cm x 40 cm) and moisten them thoroughly. Divide the fish mixture into 6 parts and roll up in the paper to make salami shaped rolls.

Put all the ingredients for the stock into a large pot, cover, bring to boil and simmer for half an hour. Add the wrapped fish rolls. They should be cooked gently for two hours.

**TIP:** To freeze gefilte fish, first wrap in foil and then in a plastic bag. Freeze the stock separately.

**TIP:** Can be prepared in smaller amounts, but for Pesach, preparing large quantities may save further work and effort during the holiday.

## MOCK FISH (FALSHE FISH)

1 kg ground chicken breast

1 chopped onion

4 tablespoons potato starch

2 eggs

salt and pepper to taste

Mix all ingredients together well.

**STOCK**

4 cups water

2 onions

3 carrots

2 parsnips

4 sugar cubes

1/2 teaspoon salt

pinch of pepper

Peel the vegetables and cut into pieces. Put into a pot with the dry ingredients and the water. Bring to a boil, cover, and simmer for 30 minutes. Form the meat mixture into medium-sized balls and add to the stock. Cook for one hour.
Can be served hot or cold.

Those who do not eat fish on Pesach, can replace it with "falshe fish."

## PESACHDIGE EGG WITH ONION

5 hard-boiled eggs

1 onion

3 medium potatoes, boiled and peeled

salt and pepper to taste

oil

Mash the eggs and potatoes using a potato masher. Chop the onion finely and add to mixture together with some oil, salt and pepper.

## CREAM OF VEGETABLE SOUP

1 kg zucchini

1 kg potatoes

1/2 celery root

1 parsnip

1 turnip

1 onion

1 clove garlic

10 cups water

salt and pepper to taste

Peel the vegetables. Cut the zucchini and potatoes into small pieces. Put all the ingredients into a large pot, bring to a boil, cover, and cook gently for an hour. Remove the parsnip and turnip and blend the rest.

*Oma's bubbelach*
*Mock fish (falshe fish)*
*Borsht*
*Matzo torte*

## OMA'S BUBBELACH

5 large potatoes

salt and pepper to taste

5 eggs, separated

Peel and boil the potatoes, then drain and mash immediately. Add salt, pepper and egg yolks and mix. In another bowl, whisk the egg whites until very stiff and fold into the potato mixture. Heat some oil in a frying pan and drop large spoonfuls of the mixture into the oil. Fry until brown on both sides.

Bubbelach can be served in a soup or as a snack, sprinkled with sugar.

This was my mother-in-law's recipe, and on Pesach, Oma's bubbelach are always a real treat for the children.

# CHICKEN KNEIDLACH

1 kg ground chicken and turkey, mixed

2 eggs

2 carrots, peeled and grated

2 boiled potatoes, mashed

2 large onions

salt and pepper to taste

*Method 1*

Chop the onions finely and sauté in a little oil. Mix together with the rest of the ingredients to a firm consistency and form into balls. Add to boiling soup and cook for half an hour.

*Method 2*

Bring 8 cups of water to a boil with 6 chicken wings, 6 chicken necks, salt and pepper to taste, and any soup vegetables desired. Cook for an hour, add the kneidlach and cook for another thirty minutes.

**TIP:** This liquid can be saved and used as a soup stock.

For those who do not eat matzo meal kneidlach, these chicken kneidlach are an ideal alternative to serve with your soup. Children will especially love very small ones.

## MATZO MEAL KNEIDLACH

5 eggs
5 tablespoons oil
salt and pepper to taste
1 1/2 cups matzo meal

Mix all ingredients together and set aside for several hours. Boil up a large pan of salted water. Wet your hands and form into small balls, then add them to the boiling water. Cook for half an hour. Serve in soup. Can also be drained and fried on both sides in a little oil and served as a side dish to meat.

## PESACH NOODLES

4 eggs
1/2 cup potato starch
1/3 cup water
pinch of salt

Mix the water, potato starch and salt together and eliminate any lumps. Add the eggs. Heat a little oil in a pan and fry large, very thin pancakes, one at a time. Add a little oil to the pan after each pancake. Roll three pancakes together and with a sharp knife cut into fine strips. Serve in soup like noodles.
Freezes very well.

## BORSHT

10 large beets
1 large onion
10 cups water
3/4 cup sugar
1/2 cup lemon juice
2 teaspoons salt
4 eggs

Peel the beets and cut into small pieces. Put the beets and a whole peeled onion in a large pot with water. Cover and cook for one hour. Add the sugar, salt and lemon juice and cook another half an hour. Remove from the heat and leave to cool for at least one hour. Remove the pieces of beetroot and the onion. Beat the eggs and whisk into the borsht. Serve cold.

**TIP:** Can be frozen.

## MAYONNAISE

1 egg
yolk of one hard-boiled egg
1 level teaspoon sugar
1/2 teaspoon salt
pinch of pepper
2 tablespoons lemon juice
2 1/2 cups oil

Blend all the ingredients in a blender except the oil. Add the oil slowly in small quantities and keep on blending. If the mayonnaise becomes too thick, add a tablespoon of boiling water.

## MATZO TORTE

10 matzos

wine

chocolate spread

(see index)

My Bubbe Taube used to serve this delicacy after Pesach, before bread became available.

Dip matzo into wine and cover with chocolate spread. Put another dipped matzo on top and spread with more chocolate. Repeat until finished. Spread the top matzo with chocolate too and sprinkle with ground almonds. Cut into squares.

**TIP:** As a variation, the matzos can be dipped into orange juice instead of wine.

## ZUCCHINI

1 kg zucchini
1 onion
oil
salt and pepper to taste
3 eggs

Chop the onion finely and sauté in a little oil. Peel the zucchini, grate coarsely and add to the pan. Sauté for half an hour. Beat the eggs with a little salt and pepper and mix into the zucchini. Cook for another 10 minutes.

**TIP:** As a variation, the eggs can be replaced by a small can of tomato paste and sugar to taste.

## CARROT TZIMMES

1/2 kg carrots
2 tablespoons sugar
1/4 teaspoon salt
3 tablespoons oil

Peel the carrots and slice into rings. Heat the oil in a pan, toss in the carrots and sauté for 15 minutes. Add the sugar and salt and cook for a further 15 minutes.

## PESACH CHOLENT

3/4 kg beef or turkey, cubed

5 large potatoes peeled and quartered

2 onions, peeled

2 large whole potatoes, peeled

1 tablespoon sugar

oil

salt, pepper and paprika

2 cups water

Carmelize the sugar in the oil. Add the cubed meat and the whole onions. Cover and cook over low heat for 1 1/2 hours taking care that it does not burn! Add the quartered potatoes, pepper, salt and paprika together with the water. Grate the two whole potatoes coarsely and add to the pan. Cook for another hour.

Before Shabbos, heat and place on a Shabbos hotplate without adding water.

## GOULASH

1 kg beef goulash

2 onions

2 or 3 cloves of garlic

3 carrots

1 zucchini

Slice the onion and the garlic into rings and sauté gently in a pan with a little oil.
Add the meat cubes and brown.
Slice the carrots and add to the pan, cover and simmer very gently for two hours.
Slice the zucchini and add, then leave to simmer, covered, for approximately an hour until ready. Serve with mashed potatoes.
The garlic can be left out if preferred.

## MEAT PATTIES

1/2 kg ground beef
1/2 kg ground veal
2 eggs
2 potatoes
salt, pepper and
paprika to taste

Peel and grate the potatoes finely. Mix all the ingredients together and form into flat patties. Fry on both sides in hot oil. Optional: You can fry a finely chopped onion and add to the mixture.

**TIP:** Freezes well. These meat patties are very suitable for taking on trips, picnics, etc.

## PESACHDIGE SCHNITZEL

chicken breast fillets
egg
salt and pepper
ground almonds

Beat the egg and mix with salt and pepper. Dip the meat in the egg and then in ground almonds. Fry on both sides in hot oil. Serve hot.

## CHICKEN À L'ORANGE

1 chicken, quartered
4 orange slices
1/4 cup orange juice
paprika

Sprinkle the chicken quarters with paprika. Lay in a baking pan with a slice of orange on each piece. Pour the orange juice over the chicken and bake for 1 3/4 hours in a preheated oven at 200°C.

## CHICKEN IN WINE

1 chicken, quartered
3 fine leeks
2 carrots
2 onions
2 cloves garlic
oil
salt, pepper, paprika to taste
1/4 cup white wine

Brown the chicken in a little oil. Remove from the pan and sprinkle with paprika. Cut the white part of the leeks, carrots, onion and garlic into thin slices and put into a pan with salt and pepper. Place the chicken on the vegetables, cover, and cook gently for 1 1/2 hours. Add the wine and cook for another 30 minutes.

**TIP:** You can thicken the sauce by stirring in a tablespoon of potato starch mixed with a tablespoon of cold water.

## CHICKEN IN THE OVEN

1 chicken, quartered
paprika
2 onions
oil

Chop the onions and sauté in oil. Place the chicken in a baking pan and sprinkle with paprika. Put a spoonful of fried onion on each piece of chicken. Bake in a preheated oven at 180°C for 1 3/4 hours.

## CARROT KUGEL

600 g carrots
600 g potatoes
2 tablespoons sugar
pinch of salt
2 eggs

Peel the carrots and leave whole. Peel the potatoes and cut into pieces. Boil the vegetables in a pot of water with a spoonful of salt until the potatoes are cooked and the carrots are half-cooked. Remove the carrots from the water. Drain the potatoes and return to flame to dry for a few moments, then mash them. Grate the carrots coarsely, and add to potatoes with the rest of the ingredients. Pour into a greased pan and bake in a preheated oven at 180°C for 1 1/4 hours.

# AUNTIE AIDEL'S APPLE JAM

1 kg sour cooking apples
(Rennet)

750 g sugar

juice of one lemon

Peel and core the apples, removing and keeping the seeds. Cut the apples into pieces and put into a pan with the sugar, lemon juice and seeds. Cook overnight (10 hours) on the lowest possible flame, with a heat diffuser if available. Half an hour before finishing, blend with a soup blender and then return to the heat. Keep refrigerated.

**NOTE:** The apple seeds are necessary to help gel the jam, instead of pectin.

## APPLE KUGEL

10 eggs

12 tablespoons sugar

juice of 1/2 a lemon

12 tablespoons boiled and coarsely mashed potatoes

4 cooking apples (Rennet), peeled and coarsely grated

cinnamon

5 tablespoons potato starch (optional)

Whisk the eggs with the sugar until stiff. Add the lemon juice, potatoes, apples and cinnamon (and potato starch if used).
Pour into greased pan. Bake in preheated oven at 180°C for 1 1/2 hours.

## ORANGE SQUASH CONCENTRATE

2 cups fresh orange juice

2 cups lemon juice

1 kg sugar

Boil the juices with the sugar until it has completely dissolved. Leave to cool and strain.
Keep refrigerated.

# APPLE BLINTZES

For basic recipe for batter,
see Pesach noodles.

**FILLING**

1/2 kg Golden Delicious
(sweet cooking) apples

2 tablespoons water

Peel the apples and cut into small pieces.
Cook for 20 minutes with the water while
stirring. Take care that they do not stick to
the pan and burn! The cooked apples
should be reduced to a thick paste. Mash
with a potato masher, add a pinch of
cinnamon, and fill the omelettes.

**SAUCE**

1 cup orange juice

1 cube sugar

1 tablespoon potato starch

Make the sauce by bringing 3/4 of the juice
to a boil with the sugar. Mix the remaining
juice with the potato starch and add to the
mixture slowly while stirring until the sauce
thickens.
Can be served hot or cold, as a dessert or
snack.

## HEARTY POTATO BLINTZES

For basic recipe for batter,
see Pesach noodles.

**FILLING**

1/2 kg potatoes, peeled

salt and pepper to taste

1 onion

oil

Boil and drain the potatoes. Chop the onions and sauté in a little oil. Mash the potatoes with a potato masher and mix with the onion and seasonings. Fill pancakes with the potato mixture. Before serving, warm up in a frying pan with a little oil.

## MATZO MEAL TORTE

5 eggs
1 1/4 cups sugar
1 cup matzo meal
1/3 cup ground almonds

Beat the eggs and the sugar until stiff. Add the matzo meal and mix. Pour the batter into a greased round or loaf pan and sprinkle with the ground almonds. Bake in a pre-heated oven at 180°C for 1 hour.

## ALMOND TART

8 eggs
250 g ground almonds
2 tablespoons cocoa or potato starch (optional)
250 g sugar

Whisk the egg yolks with some of the sugar until stiff. Add the ground almonds. Sift the cocoa, or potato starch if used, and add. In another bowl whisk the egg whites until very stiff. Add the rest of the sugar and whisk again. Gently mix the egg whites into the first mixture with a wooden spoon. Pour into a round greased pan and bake in a preheated oven at 180°C for 1 hour.

## PESACH CHOCOLATE CAKE I

14 eggs

14 tablespoons sugar

1 tablespoon oil

3 tablespoons wine

6 tablespoons potato starch

3 tablespoons cocoa powder

6 tablespoons ground almonds

Whisk the egg yolks with the sugar until stiff. Add the oil and wine while whisking. Mix the flour and cocoa together and fold in to the egg yolk mixture, followed by the almonds. Whisk the egg whites until very stiff and fold into the batter with a wooden spoon. Pour into a large greased pan and bake in a preheated oven at 180°C for 1 hour and 15 minutes.

## PESACH CHOCOLATE CAKE II

6 eggs

1 1/4 cups sugar

1/2 cup orange juice

1 tablespoon oil

1 tablespoon wine

pinch of cinnamon

pinch of salt

5 heaping tablespoons potato starch

2 tablespoons cocoa

Whisk the egg yolks with half the sugar until stiff. Slowly add the juice, oil, wine, cinnamon and salt while whisking. Fold in the potato starch and cocoa. Whisk the egg whites until stiff. Slowly add the rest of the sugar while whisking. Fold the egg whites into the batter. Pour into two greased 25 cm loaf pans and bake in a preheated oven at 170° to 180°C for 1 hour and 10 minutes.

**TIP:** Two teaspoons of baking powder can be added.

## POTATO-STARCH CAKE

10 eggs
400 g sugar
200 g potato starch

Whisk the egg yolks with half the sugar until creamy. Add the flour. Set aside. Whisk the egg whites until stiff, add the rest of the sugar while whisking, and fold into the batter by hand. Bake in a large greased pan in a preheated oven at 180°C for 1 hour and 15 minutes.

## ALMOND AND POTATO-STARCH CAKE

14 eggs
14 tablespoons sugar
juice of one lemon
6 tablespoons potato starch
12 tablespoons ground almonds

Whisk the egg yolks with the sugar until stiff. Add the potato starch, almonds and lemon juice. Whisk the egg whites until stiff and fold in by hand. Pour into a large greased pan and bake in a preheated oven at 180°C for 1 hour and 15 minutes.

## COCONUT FLAVORED CAKE

15 eggs
600 g sugar
200 g potato starch
100 g dried coconut
pinch of salt

Whisk the egg yolks with two thirds of the sugar until stiff. Fold in the coconut and the potato starch with a spatula. Whisk the egg whites until stiff and slowly add the rest of the sugar. Now carefully fold the egg whites into the coconut mixture with a spatula. Pour into three 25 cm greased loaf pans and bake in a preheated oven at 180°C for 1 hour and 15 minutes.

Although this recipe is very simple, the result is a splendid Pesach cake.

# FLUDEN

### WHITE MIXTURE

1/2 kg white (peeled)
ground almonds

350 g sugar

4 egg whites

juice of 1 lemon

2 tablespoons potato starch
(optional)

### DARK MIXTURE

1/2 kg unpeeled
ground almonds

350 g sugar

4 egg whites

juice of 1 lemon

2 tablespoons cocoa (optional)

2 tablespoons potato starch
(optional)

Mix together ingredients of each mixture well. Spread the brown mixture into a greased baking pan, approximately 20 cm x 30 cm, and then spread the white mixture on top. Preheat the oven to 180°C. Bake the fluden for approximately 1 hour and 10 minutes. or until golden brown. Leave overnight to cool before cutting into squares.

**TIP:** As a variation, each color can be baked separately, or the fluden can be made in one color only.

## MALKA'S MARZIPAN BALLS

2 cups ground
white almonds

1 cup dried coconut

3/4 cup sugar

1 tablespoon lemon juice

3 tablespoons boiling water

pinch of cinnamon

coconut for garnishing

Mix all ingredients together to make a dough. Form small balls and roll in dried coconut. Place each ball in a small cupcake paper. Keep refrigerated.

## OMA OLLECH'S ALMOND MACAROONS

2 egg whites

100 g sugar

110 g finely ground almonds

50 g coarsely ground walnuts

a few drops of lemon juice

pinch of cinnamon

Whisk the egg whites until stiff. Add the sugar slowly while beating. Fold in the rest of the ingredients with a spatula. Drop heaping teaspoonfuls of the mixture onto a greased baking tray well apart to allow for spreading. Bake in a preheated oven at 125°C for 1 1/4 hours.

## ALMOND COOKIES

1/2 kg ground almonds

4 egg whites

350 g sugar

juice of 1 lemon

pinch of cinnamon

blanched almond halves
for garnishing

Combine all ingredients to make a dough. Wet your hands and form into small balls. Press an almond half into each ball. Bake in a preheated oven at 160°C for approximately 30 minutes.

## COCONUT COOKIES

4 egg whites

200 g sugar

250 g dried coconut

2 heaping tablespoons
potato starch

a few drops of lemon juice

Whisk the egg whites until very stiff. Slowly add the sugar while beating. Carefully fold in the coconut and potato starch with a spatula, and then add the lemon juice. Line a baking tray with baking parchment. Drop teaspoonfuls of the mixture onto the tray. Bake in a preheated oven at 175°C for 15 minutes. The cookies should remain light in color, as they tend to become hard as they darken.

## CHOCOLATE SPREAD

1 egg
125 g butter
1/2 cup sugar
1 packet vanilla sugar
2 tablespoons cocoa
pinch of cinnamon

Blend all ingredients together well.
Refrigerate.

# Notes

# INDEX

# I N D E X